KU-739-276

Christ in the Classroom

CHRIST
in the Classroom

by F. J. Sheed

SHEED AND WARD

London   New York

Library of Congress Cataloging in Publication Data

Sheed, Francis Joseph, 1897–
  Christ in the classroom.

  Bibliography: p.
  1. Jesus Christ—Person and offices. 2. Christian
life—Catholic authors. 3. Religious education.
I. Title.
BT202.S47   1973   232   739–952
ISBN 0–8362–0523–5

Nihil Obstat: James A. O'Donohoe

Imprimatur: ✠ Humberto S. Medeiros
              Archbishop of Boston

Date: January 26, 1973

Contents

Introductory

About twenty years ago the Conference of Teaching Nuns of Ireland asked me to talk to them on the question Are We Really Teaching Religion? The talk was published as a pamphlet bearing that title. It was widely read, its relevance not questioned.

Then came Pope John. We are living in a different Catholic world. Teachers are different, pupils are even more different. At the heart of the difference is that one can no longer take for granted any special interest in Christ. Being asked by Bishop Pursley to talk on Catechetics to the priests of Fort Wayne diocese, I chose as title The Catechetics of Jesus. That talk is expanded into this present book.

It is not about the teaching of the Faith in general. It is concerned solely with Jesus as the young may be helped to know him and grow in intimacy with him. Only as he himself is known can Trinity and Incarnation and Redemption, life here and hereafter, Church and Sacraments, be intelligently accepted—or even intelligently rejected!

It is concerned directly with teaching either in Catholic schools or in the classes of such bodies as the Confraternity of Christian Doctrine. I hope it may also help parents who wish to help their children grow in wisdom and understanding, to say nothing of grace with God and men.

Teaching apart, it might be a useful refresher course for any who have let their Redeemer fade too far into the back of the mind.

Long ago I presumed to advise a group of young men on their way to the priesthood: "Make up your mind whether you are preaching Christ or yourself. If it's yourself, heaven help you. For the better you do, the worse it is." I would give the same kind of advice to teachers of religion.

F. J. S.

I

A Sort of Survey

The general object of education is to prepare the pupils for life. The teacher examining his conscience in moments of insomnia might ask himself: "What responses to the truth and beauty of reality have I developed in my pupils today? Have I mutilated any, killed any?"

The special object of religious education is to prepare the pupils for life in Christ. For the teacher, the test is how they are responding to Christ—not only are they growing in their knowledge of him, but what in fact does he mean to them and how intensely does he mean it? How is the teacher to find out? Certainly no examination can tell him. But as they enter their last year in the primary school, he might ask them to write down their thoughts on two questions—with a month or so between: "What difference if Jesus had not come?" "What difference did his dying make?" As they enter their last year in high school, the same questions could be put to them, but with an emphasis on the difference to *themselves*. A profitable hour might be spent in discussing the answers with the class.

The Dimming of Jesus

Jesus Hardly Known

My own experience suggests that the results of such an experiment might be hair-raising. Two or three years ago I asked several hundred first- and second-year boys and girls of a Catholic high school, "What is the point of going to Mass?" At the end of forty minutes discussion, they could not think of anything gained by going or lost by staying away. At a separate session I asked several hundred third- and fourth-year students if there was any point in being a Catholic. They could not think of any. What was specially notable in each session was that no one mentioned Jesus till I did.

Wherever I go I find an evaporation of belief in him among the thirteen- to thirty-year-olds, and a dimming of belief at all ages and all levels. People who would be horrified to have their faith in Jesus questioned do not in fact find him very interesting, do not seem to find their minds naturally turning to him in their daily living, do not think of death as bringing them closer to him. One can almost feel his absence everywhere. I select three points at which it is especially hard not to feel it.

1. In all the arguments about the new Mass—Latin or vernacular, vestments or overalls, organ or guitars, church or kitchen table—I have never heard Our Lord mentioned.

2. Of the accounts given of themselves by priests who have moved out of the Church I have read more than most because I travel more. I can hardly remember one in which he is so much as referred to—yet not only to the Mass they had said daily but to all their priestly lives he gave whatever meaning there was. Often enough Mass and the rest have lost their meaning for them: but it is odd that

it does not occur to them to tell us how this affects their relation with Jesus.

3. In a twenty-five column dialogue conducted by the editor of a Catholic weekly with half a dozen graduates of Catholic colleges about the present condition of the Church (lamentable) and the possibility of its renewal (minimal), Our Lord was mentioned three times and dropped immediately, he rated under half a column. In a long and brilliant article I have just read by a black Catholic on whether there is a future for her race within the Church, Jesus is not mentioned.

I could go on and on. But there is one piece of evidence available to the Mass-going Catholic fifty times or so a year —namely, the sermons. There are indeed comments on the Gospel of the day, but one practically never hears a sermon directly about Jesus himself: indeed one rarely hears anything that could be new to any twelve-year-old in the congregation. No contrast could be more glaring than between what the religious syllabus says has been taught in school and what the sermons assume has been learnt.

OUR PRESENT CONFUSIONS

Till twenty years ago the Catholic teacher thought he knew who and what Christ was. He had the theology of the Incarnation, as built up by the definitions of Nicea, Ephesus, Chalcedon; there were the Gospels to give the God-man's redeeming life on earth. Now he is not so sure. He has the Scripture critics, Catholics among them, who leave him wondering whether the Gospels can tell him anything at all about Jesus. There are theologians, Catholics among them, questioning every word of the standard teaching on who or what he was. Not that there is a newly emergent Jesus, accepted by the majority of scholars, to set against the Jesus of the centuries. Every expert makes his own choice, builds his own Jesus, interpreting in the light of his own philosophy of life as much of Scripture as he still finds acceptable. At present the confusion verges on the chaotic. But there is careful study going on and brilliant thinking inside the Church and out, the Holy Spirit has not abandoned his people; the Second Vatican Council has emphasized the way of growth in the light. The chaos will settle, and we shall be seeing Christ's revelation with new clarity, at a new depth.

But it has not settled yet. What is the ordinary Catholic to do meanwhile? Hear every point of view, then make his own decision? But if even the specialist who does nothing else couldn't possibly read everything, how is the plain Christian to decide? He has not the equipment—he does not know the traditional theology, he has not the scholarship to weigh the arguments. What *can* he do? He can

(a) pick some teacher—far right, far left or center—whose writing or speaking appeals to him;

(b) forget the whole thing, stick to Mass and Communion till the chaos settles down.

So much for the plain man. What is the Catholic teacher to do? A chaos is suitable for writing about to special readers and lecturing about to special audiences. It is not suitable for teaching, least of all to beginners. It may be that for an individual teacher the chaos is indeed settling, that he is seeing a line growing continually clearer; but he is still feeling his way, questioning at every point, testing and discarding, and testing again. Each teacher might, of course, decide how much he himself is convinced of and teach that, but

(a) convictions are not particularly valuable for being his—most of us are nobody in particular;

(b) other teachers will believe more or believe less, and only confusion can result;

(c) parents have sent their children to a Catholic class to learn what the Church teaches, not what Teacher A thinks or Teacher B. If they want Private Judgment, there are Churches in which it belongs.

The Catholic Church is a teaching Church—its Founder commissioned it to make all nations its disciples, "teaching them to observe all I have commanded you." The schools and the Confraternity of Christian Doctrine classes are provided by her and cannot well be used to contradict what she teaches. For there *is* a standard Catholic doctrine. There are definitions, issuing from centuries of living Christ's revelation, thinking about it and praying about it, and opening the way to further defining. Vatican II has at once clarified and reaffirmed the Church's teaching function. In the statement on Religious Freedom (para. 14) we read: "It is her duty authoritatively to teach the Truth which is Christ himself and also to declare and confirm by her authority those principles of the moral law which have their origin in human nature itself." But in Ecumenism (para. 6) it states the principle that "if the influence of events or the times has led to deficiencies in conduct, in Church discipline, *or even in the formulation of doctrine* (which must be carefully distinguished from the deposit of Faith itself) these should be appropriately rectified."

Ultimately, one supposes, the Catholic teaching authority in each area will decide what should be taught in its classes. Which does not mean that the teachers should close their eyes and their ears to the discussion which fills the air. They must be aware of it for their own mental growth, they must be aware of it for the sake of their students—at any rate those in college and the seniors in high school, who also hear about it and read about it. But if either they or their students are to gain anything from it, they must know Jesus as the Gospels show him. With that knowledge rooted in them and growing towards intimacy, they can proceed to a consideration of what the Scripture scholars have to offer them, to say nothing of the theologians and the teaching Church.

JESUS IN THE CLASSROOM

Too often Jesus is simply an item in the syllabus, to be discussed when the syllabus reaches him, and then only till it passes on to the next topic. The Faith is presented as a package deal (Jesus in with the rest) to be accepted whole; the trouble is that what can be accepted whole can be rejected whole. Religion should be so taught that even if they reject the rest, he will be seen as distinct, it will not occur to them to reject him along with the rest as a matter of course. If they hold on to him by so much as a fingertip, he can do things in their souls.

As an item in the syllabus, how has he been presented? Mainly, I fancy, as a piece in the theological diagram of Redemption, as Man indeed, but not as that particular man; as Man with a body and soul, the soul quasi-infinite, the body fresh-minted for him. But he was "the fruit of David's loins," says Peter; "the seed of David according to the flesh," says Paul. So was his Mother—forty generations of ancestors back to David, how many back to the beginning of the race? He got the body that came to him from his ancestors, as we all do—each of us, he and we, having our own individual likes and dislikes, attractions and repulsions, things found easy and things found difficult: he was tempted as we are, but without sin as we are not.

Young Christians must see him, not as one of his own statues galvanized, walking the road to Calvary majestically, but as a living man with his own individual reactions. They should study him at least as closely as they would study Abraham Lincoln in the history class, Hamlet in the English class. Without that there is no relating to him, no genuine encounter; intimacy with him is not even thinkable.

The Teacher

Whatever their subject, all teachers live in the certainty that every lapse is going to be exaggerated. This is annoying, but in most subjects it does not greatly matter: no student is going to be less devoted to algebra or history because a teacher lost his temper too often or pretended to know what he didn't. But every fault of the religion teacher is charged against the Faith: many a fallen-away Catholic is taking his revenge on some teacher of long ago. To an appalling extent the religion teacher cannot help representing the Faith. This means that three qualifications are essential: he must be interested in Our Lord, must know at least the Gospels, must be interested in the minds of his pupils.

1. The teacher must be interested in Jesus. If this sounds so obvious to you as to be not worth saying, then you were very fortunate in your teachers. I remember a story of a teacher in a country where Scripture had to be taught in the State schools. He happened not to believe a word of it. Being a conscientious man, he did his best. Having to instruct his class on the Feeding of the Five Thousand, he concentrated on the twelve baskets of crumbs and drew the moral that Christ wanted the school yard kept tidy.

But it is not of unbelievers I am thinking, though there are Catholic teachers who believe little enough. I am concerned with that boredom with religion which is spreading like a blight over the Christian world. I get the feeling that many priests are devoting themselves to Civil Rights (a cause admirable in itself) simply because they are bored with God—a continuance, perhaps, of their seminary boredom with theology seen as a series of obstacles to be hurdled on their way to ordination, of no practical importance for souls.

A teacher will be able to introduce the young into the

world of the Faith only if he is living in it himself and rejoicing to live in it, just as he will teach more vividly the geography of a country he has visited and loved.

It is my conviction that a teacher who finds the Faith uninteresting is bound in conscience to ask to be excused from teaching it.

2. The teacher must know the Gospels.   Evidently he cannot make much of the Gospels unless he knows a great deal more, both within the two Testaments and outside them. But I concentrate here on the Gospels, on Matthew, Mark, Luke and John as men have met Jesus in them for nineteen centuries. The teacher should know them at least as well as he would *Hamlet* if he were preparing his pupils for an examination—in the religion class he is preparing them for an examination more searching, of effect more far-reaching. I remember asking the principal of a Catholic school why she left Doctrine to be taught by teachers who would not have been allowed to teach any other subject of which they knew so little. She answered, "Well, you see, the children's careers don't depend on it." (They don't, don't they?)

I take a handful of examples of insufficient Gospel knowledge. There was the preacher who said how suitable that Jesus should have entrusted his Mother to John because John had no mother of his own—whereas Matthew tells us that John's mother was actually there on Calvary. I remember an occasion when, commenting on Paul's words "God sent his son born of a woman," I remarked that Our Lady is the only person, human or divine, who could say to God the Father, "Your Son and mine." A teacher in the audience asked, "Couldn't the Holy Spirit?"

Errors of this sort startle. But there is another kind of defect in reading which does not startle because it does not amount to error actually uttered. Of sermons I have heard on the parable of the Pharisee and the Publican I have kept no count: but I do know that in not a single one of them was it mentioned that one of the Twelve who heard the parable had been a publican himself.

That, you may say, is merely a failure to bring two pieces of knowledge together, at worst a sin of omission. But it suggests that the Gospel story is not really being "seen" by the preacher. In this instance, of course, the point at issue is not of great importance. Consider another. When Peter urged Jesus not to suffer and die, Jesus said to him, "Get behind me, Satan." But in Gethsemane he prayed to his Father that he might not drink the cup. Was he asking God for something which he called Satanic when Peter first suggested it? The question goes to the root of our Redemption. I have never met a lay Catholic who had even heard it raised.

3. The teacher must be interested in his pupils, especially in their minds. One remembers Winston Churchill's definition of a fanatic: a man who cannot change his mind and will not change the subject. The fanatic is profoundly interested in his theme, but not in his hearers: they are supporters to be won, or merely an audience he simply has to have. A teacher of this sort might know his subject thoroughly and expound it clearly, yet be a crashing bore. The religion teacher must be wholly aware of his hearers as taking a genuine part in a true dialogue: and this not only in order to hold their attention, but principally because there is no real teaching without it.

In all subjects that are going to affect the conduct of life, it is a mere truism that teaching does not consist in the utterance of information, however valuable. The essence of teaching is communication, and the way of it is to effect a union of minds, in the hope that a reality living in one mind may become a reality living in the other. There is a real analogy here with the life-giving union of bodies. The second person should be not simply a receiver but must respond fully, the first not simply a conveyer but concerned with the other's response and responsive to it. For perfection of either union there must be love: or at least that beginning of love which includes an interest in the other as himself, an interest in his response, a care *for his sake* how he responds. Certainly the student will not take anything from a teacher he dislikes. All this talk of union of minds may sound grandiose, but it is the minimum, there is no effective teaching of religion without it. It flows from this that any slackness in preparing the lesson, any want of wholeheartedness in giving it, is a way of taking the name of God in vain.

The System

In Catholic schools very great difficulty arises for the teacher of religion, in that religion has to be taught in the same building, on the same timetable, by the same men and women, as all the other subjects. It is a pity not only because the students will almost inevitably tend to think of religion as one more lesson, to be dropped with all the others when they leave school: an impression only confirmed if there are examinations in Religious Knowledge, with marks and grades and credits, just like all the rest. Teachers tell me that there is no way of getting students to take seriously a subject in which there is no examination. I can only hope they will find one. Short of that, they must find some way of getting the students to feel that examinations in religion are at least different from all others. For it is in everyone's nature to want to leave school behind. St. Paul talks of Christian maturity as "putting away the things of a child": too many Catholics list St. Paul himself as one of the childish things to be put away.

But a profounder problem arises from the teaching of

religion in school, a problem for the teacher himself. In the religion class he has a different role, has almost to be a different person. The authority he brings to other classes has no meaning in this. Here he is simply an older member of the Mystical Body given the privilege of helping younger members (who do not appreciate the privilege!) to come to maturity in the life of the Body. If to anyone this sounds pretentious, he has missed the point. It is elementary.

Most teachers can't make the adjustment, most pupils can't take the adjustment. Therefore ideally the religion teacher should not be the same teacher as handles that particular class most of the day. With the best teacher-relation, there can hardly fail to be individual resentments, with students on the teacher's nerves, the teacher on theirs. It is not easy for a teacher to go from being a tiger in the algebra class to being a lamb in the religion class. The situation is worse if the class is the tiger and the teacher gets the mauling. It would be best if the religion class were taken by a teacher who had been fraying the nerves of—and having his nerves frayed by—other classes during the rest of the day!

Where the class is being conducted by the Confraternity of Christian Doctrine the problems are different. The teacher brings no resentment from conflicts in other classes, but if it is held outside ordinary school hours he may have to contend with the resentment of the students, all of them, at having to be there at all. If it is in the school as part of the regular timetable, then once more religion can seem to be a school subject, to be left behind with school. Either way, the C.C.D. teacher, unless he happens to be a schoolteacher himself, is not likely to have the same skill in handling a pack of girls and boys.

No, it is not easy. But even if the one teacher has to teach religion and secular subjects to the same class he must do his best to remember that God is love. However efficiently doctrine and ritual may be explained, if at the end of all the young do not see religion as essentially love of God and love of man, then the school has failed them.

It would be wonderful if the students could say "Even Sister So and So is kind in religion class." That may be too much to hope. But at least Sister So and So should watch her ways more carefully when she is helping her students to a deeper intimacy with Jesus than with French grammar. I remember a school which, during the Second World War, decided to have a Novena for Peace fifteen minutes before the start of the school day. Mother Superior herself stood at the door to box the ears of children who did not arrive on time to pray for peace.

That sort of eccentricity can be controlled. But there is one continuing temptation for the teacher of any age or sex on any subject, indeed for anyone in authority over anyone. I mean sarcasm. It can be sheer cruelty—like a small boy tearing the wings off a fly or like a big man hitting a little man. As between two beings made in the image of God it is inexcusable. In one who believes that God is love it is sheer lunacy. There was the daily communicant father, for instance, who came back to breakfast to pour out his sarcasm on his children: I need hardly add that his sons are out of the Church. Teachers may have one excuse for sarcasm not available to others, namely that their nerves can be so frayed from the daylong contest with beasts wilder than those Paul was up against at Ephesus: sarcasm is a safety valve for men sometimes on the point of screaming. I know because in my youth I taught school, sometimes barely holding on to my sanity against the ways of cussedness open to the young. All the same, the teacher of religion must keep reminding himself that his sarcasm is added to all the obstacles that already stand between the student and the love of God, and that it was he who put it there.

It follows also from the special function of the teacher as an older member of the Mystical Body helping a younger towards maturity in Christ, that the ordinary school punishments have no place in the religion class. The discipline should be no more than is required to keep the class functioning—rather like that of a sensible adult at a school picnic. If the young are daydreaming, the teacher must learn to be more interesting than their dreams.

So far I have been assuming that the class may include a proportion who are bored with religion but not actively hostile—like the boy in a Catholic high school where I was lecturing, who referred to the Mass as "all that flummery at the altar." There are hostile ones too. Even more than the bored ones they need the Faith. If they join in the questioning with respect for the beliefs of others, realizing that the class is not a battleground but a meeting of minds, their presence could be valuable—to themselves, perhaps to the others as they meet here in class an attitude they will constantly encounter in the world. The teacher will still have to find a mean between welcoming their contribution to the discussion and letting them monopolize it. If they are violently hostile, they can make a shambles of the discussion class. I do not pretend that I have the answer.

To summarize: The rule for teachers should be St. Paul's rule for fathers: "Don't provoke your children to anger, lest they become discouraged." Paul says it twice, to the Colossians (3.21) and to the Ephesians (6.4). Oddly enough, I have never heard it mentioned in the pulpit.

I come now to a matter in which I have not enough experience. I merely suggest to those who have to make decisions in this area that five religion classes a week are too many. By the end of high school the students will have had over two thousand religion classes. My own notion would be two a week. I am referring, of course, to direct verbal teaching of Doctrine and Scripture. To the application of these to daily life as it now is—Civil Rights, for instance—and to non-verbal ways of teaching like audio-visual aids, as many hours may be given as seem good.

In the two classes directly concerned with Doctrine and Scripture, I suggest that in one the teacher should do his teaching, in the other the class should discuss what he has taught. In the instruction class there might be as much dialogue, in the discussion class as much summarization by himself, as the teacher finds useful. The discussion might begin with a six- or seven-minute talk by a different member of the class each week. This would help to fill one vast gap in the formation of the Catholic. In my fifty-year contact with religion in schools, there has been a general improvement in what is taught. But I hardly ever meet a Catholic who at school had been taught *utterance*—to talk as freely and intelligently about Christ as about politics or sport. Only if all who believe in him can learn to talk of him like that is there any possibility of bringing him back into a world which sees him so dimly.

DISCUSSION

The teacher who has never seen a theological or moral difficulty himself will not be of much use. He will be a great deal worse than useless if he throttles the thinking minds of his class with dogmatic answers. (Mixed metaphor? It is indeed.) He will teach best the truths with which his own mind has had to wrestle. Long ago I was asked to give some lectures at a teachers' college. At the end the principal said to me, "You have questioned our most fundamental principles." I said, "Haven't you?" It was inexcusably rude of me. But there is a moral in it for every teacher.

Spirit

The Catholic teacher may have been brought up to take "spirit" for granted—"God is spirit," says Christ. But

Christ does not define spirit for us. The catechism does, of course. But if the teacher has not gone deep into the formulas of the catechism, he is not equipped to instruct anyone in the Faith.

For spirit is basic to every topic in the religion class. The students do not need to be reminded that they have bodies, but spirit they can totally overlook. The teacher must bring his whole mind to bear on it, always thinking of ways of making the idea clearer to the students, feeling that he could find better ways.

It involves the use of mental muscles the students are not much called upon to use. Like most of us they do most of their thinking not with the intellect but with the memory, the imagination, the will, the blood, the stomach. The teacher must massage the muscles they think with, stir them into action—reluctant action at first, but with a growing excitement in it, as their exercise brings suppleness and competence. Even the bored or unconvinced members of the class can be caught by the intellectual interest of the discussion, if they feel they are really being brought into it, and not simply preached at.

By sixteen or seventeen the students should have a grasp on the concept of spirit not only as the being which can know and love but in its essential distinction from matter. It is simple, not complex: that is to say it has no parts as material things have: there is no element in a spirit which is not the whole of it. Help them to see that this means that it has a permanent hold upon what it is, can be only itself. They may not see this quickly. It is worth striving for. In every year the ideas *as stateable* should have grown richer and clearer. Not only that, but spirit itself will have been *lived with*, leading to an intimacy with the idea of it deeper than words or concepts can express. Spirit can become an essential element in the world they are mentally living in, so that world and thinking alike would be thin and impoverished without it.

To minds thus matured, materialism (however persuasively presented) would at once be seen as repulsive: it would find all their mental habits ranged solidly against it: just as, if a man has learned to walk, the most persuasive arguments could not get him to go on all fours, he would find the idea repulsive, all his bodily and mental habits would be ranged against it. And materialism, with all its emphasis on the body, sees no future for it, dooms it to sink back into the mindlessness of matter. For the Christian the body is an essential element in the whole man: it will rise from death and have its own splendor everlastingly.

(Many sentences in these last paragraphs are quoted from *Are We Really Teaching Religion?* I have discussed the whole topic in more detail in *God and the Human Mind* and in *Genesis Regained*.)

I have spent some time on the Discussion of Spirit, partly because of the importance of the topic, partly as drawing attention to the principles to be observed in the meeting of minds between teacher and class.

Intellect and Imagination

We have noted the difficulty with which our intellect functions. Its principal antagonist is imagination. Imagination is our power of making mental pictures of the material universe. What we have experienced through our senses—sights, sounds, tastes, scents, contacts—can be reproduced in the imagination, either as they originally came through the senses or in any variety of combinations. It is a marvellous, enriching power, life would be impoverished without it; but it is subordinate and is limited to the world of matter. What cannot be experienced through the senses cannot be pictured by the imagination. But it can interfere with the intellect, in two ways principally—as censor and as substitute. It will be useful to let the students see the difficulties we ourselves have had in keeping imagination under control.

As censor, imagination refuses to let us accept any statement it cannot cope with. Tell a man that his soul has no shape, size, color or weight and he dismisses it as unimaginable. Which indeed it is. Because spiritual reality is beyond the reach of the senses. You can see a just man, you can see him acting justly, but justice you cannot see.

In this area the word "imaginable" has no function: the word you want is "conceivable." If a statement does not contradict known reality, if it contains no contradiction with itself, then you can conceive it.

The word "unimaginable" is usually taken as final, the notion is to be rejected. But the Christian finds all sorts of unimaginable beliefs that he cannot just drop. At that point imagination moves in from a different angle: it offers to help intellect to accept the unimaginable doctrines *with mental pictures from the world of matter.* For the doctrine of the Trinity it substitutes a shamrock, or a triangle, or three drops of water poured together to form one drop. There is a role for such analogies in clarifying God's dealings with men, but they shed no light upon God's own being, or upon the meaning of spirit. They do not help us to see the reality, but only to swallow the doctrine. We must be sure that our students do not confuse the unimaginable with the inconceivable. In that distinction, realized and practiced, lies the way to mental maturity, a useful companion to that commoner phenomenon bodily maturity.

P.S. on Maturity. The teacher knows that the students are immature, knows too that they would be furious if he told them so. He might blunt their fury and even win their partial agreement if he explains. (a) He does not say that they are necessarily less mature than he or any other elder, only that they are less mature than they themselves are likely to be fifteen years from now. Maturity is not gained by staying alive for a given number of years: maturity is the response to experience; some older people have learnt nothing from what life has done to them and will die barely maturer than they were born. (b) However well the young have responded, too many things have not yet happened to them. They *must* be maturer fifteen years hence; i.e., many things will look different to them—unless life will have taught them nothing.

The teacher who encourages his students to use their minds will discover that his own is getting a wonderful workout. And this will be a wholly enjoyable experience if he makes no pretense of omniscience and is not embarrassed (as in other classes he might be) to admit that he doesn't know the answer, or that a previous answer given by him was wrong, or (most testing) that a student who differed from him was right.

II

The Jesus
of the Gospels

WHY THE GOSPELS

The teacher must know the Gospels, which includes knowing why he must know them. And by the Gospels I mean Matthew, Mark, Luke and John as men have met Jesus in them through nineteen centuries. Only when these are known, as I have noted, can we understand either the teaching of the Church or the reinterpretations of the critics. He should know something of the dates at which they were probably written and the reasons for attaching the names of the evangelists to them. He should know, too, of considerations to be taken into account when reading them, considerations in which all are agreed—e.g.: (1) The order of time meant less to the evangelists than to us. They would put an event or utterance not necessarily when it happened or was said but along with related things said or done at a different time—logical fitness, not chronological. (2) Hebrew idioms have constantly to be allowed for. I take two instances: (a) numbers are frequently used not as a matter of arithmetic but of emphasis—the duty of forgiving unto 70 times 7 is a way of saying not that the 491st sin is not to be forgiven, but that there is no limit at all; (b) overstatement is used as a device to force attention—Luke (14.26) quotes Jesus as calling on us to "hate" father and mother. Hate was a colorful way of saying "love less"; and so Matthew gives it (10.37): "If you love father or mother more than me, you are not worthy of me"; and he gives the context—an issue might arise in which a man must take Jesus' side even against his family.

It is important that the teacher should be at home in each Gospel individually. Matthew's theme is Christ's kingdom as the fulfillment of God's plan for the Israel of the Old Testament: Mark's is "the beginning of the Gospel of Jesus Christ, the Son of God"—the manhood unmistakable, the Godhead showing through. According to Papias (who died in 130), Mark wrote down what he had heard Peter preach about Jesus' life and work, most richly of his personality, not much of what he actually taught, but much of what he did (remembered in detail). Luke conceived his Gospel and the Acts as one continuous treatment of his main theme—where Matthew shows the universality of the kingdom growing from Israel, Luke shows it growing into all humanity. John's Gospel tells us explicitly "these things are written that you may believe that Jesus is the Christ, the Son of God, and believing you may have life in his name": humanity, divinity, life, are John's concerns. With all this individuality, all four are portraying the one same person.

The Gospels were not written as a beginners' course, a first introduction to Christianity. Not only the evangelists, but Paul and the other New Testament writers, assume that their readers have already been instructed—they were writing to develop and enrich the teaching their readers had been given by the Church into which they had been baptized. Scripture nowhere sets out that basic instruction. But what a writer assumes his readers know is a constituent element of any book. Not knowing it, today's reader lacks what the first readers had.

The Catholic believes that in the Church Christ founded, under the guidance of the Spirit he sent, the basic teaching has been continuously taught, and lived, and phrased at new depth. There is no question of the Church *or* Scripture. They are both ways of utterance of the one God, two ways of approach to the same reality.

There are arguments among Christians as to the Church's growth in understanding of Christ's teaching, but as to the detail of his earthly life, what he did and suffered, what he said, she has made no change in the Gospels as she has had them from their first writing. Neither have those Christian Churches or individual scholars who interpret his teachings differently.

Only in the Gospels do we meet the Jesus who lived and taught and died. For all understanding of him, even to know what there is to understand, we must go to the Gospels. A non-Gospel Christ is a mere artifact, compounded of its inventor's principles, preferences, experiences, insights, prejudices—in fact, what its inventor would have been if he had been Jesus.

What the Church's theologians have given on Christ must largely be supplied by the teacher, since reading the great theologians is beyond the young. The Gospels he can help them to read, so that they can make their own discovery of the Gospel Jesus. But only if the teacher has himself found it. If he hasn't, he may be reduced to persuading them that Jesus is as interesting as such heroes—political, cinematic, athletic—as they already have.

Non-Gospel Christs

Of what I have called artifacts, pseudo-Christs, there are three main types, two of them to be found in a great deal of the teaching given to Christians throughout the ages, the third arrived more recently.

1. For vast numbers of believers, the one fact that matters about Jesus is that he loved his fellow-men. All other elements in his character have faded away into loving-kindness, so that even his love is milk-and-watered. He is gentle, meek and mild—adjectives which do not suggest the sort of man one would want in an emergency, adjectives which would have startled those who knew him in Palestine.

2. Teachers who would not be tempted to that sort of cheapening can go to a different extreme, seeing Jesus, in the sense we have already glanced at, as a piece in the diagram of Redemption. It is just too geometrical, with the Divinity and Humanity of Chalcedon's definition little more than words which merge logically into the word Redemption. The Chalcedon definition was not a blueprint but a brilliant thrust into the surrounding darkness.

3. These two ways of presenting him accept a real Jesus of Nazareth and use the Gospels at least as a starting point. But there are ways of by-passing Jesus altogether while keeping the name Christ.

There are those for whom the question whether Jesus actually did and said what the Gospels relate completely misses the point. What matters is the message, the meaning. The message of a parable, the meaning, the whole value in fact, is exactly the same whether there was or was not a Prodigal Son, say, or a Good Samaritan: so with the Gospel Jesus. But we are redeemed by what Jesus did, illumined by what he said. The critics can help us to see meaning and message more clearly, so can the theologians and the canonists: but meaning and message matter because they are Christ's.

That way of by-passing Jesus is for the scholar, the academic man. This next one is definitely not. The name of

Christ is uttered against the established order—ecclesiastical, political or economic. There is small sign that the Gospels have been closely studied. Christ is too often a slogan, a name given the ideals and indignations of the individual who uses his name.

We hear more and more of the duty of seeing Christ not in first-century Palestine but in our fellow-men. It is a vast commitment, to love others as we should love Christ, to serve others as we should serve Christ. But unless we know the first-century Christ, the Christ that actually was, what is it that we are seeing in others and calling "Christ"?

If Jesus himself fades into the back of men's minds, his message will not last: its power over men has always lain in its being his: the Gospel words live with his life, they are not just words but words issuing from one who had compassion on the multitude, who in the agony of his crucifixion begged God to forgive his torturers. What Jesus said and did is basic both to an understanding of the theology that the Church has developed and to an evaluation of the insights and reinterpretations now pouring out from the men who devote their lives to Scripture study.

To repeat, the main object of religious teaching should be to help the student, in the measure of his own personal maturing, to grow in intimacy with Jesus himself, and in understanding of the light he sheds on God and on human life.

JESUS IN THE GOSPELS

What I am trying to do in this small book is to show how the Gospels may be used for this purpose. Our study of the God from whom Jesus came forth should be based on the words the Gospels record. All the truths which come from Jesus himself—Redemption, Eternal Life, Church, doctrine, sacraments, morals—should be studied as we hear him phrase them. This applies particularly to the living of our lives and our duties to others. It is not enough to have worked out our own ideas on how life, individual or social, should be lived and garnish them with any texts in which we find him agreeing with us. This comes very close to preaching not Christ but oneself.

Teachers will decide how to cover the ground in primary schools and high schools. Provided it has been thoroughly covered, the same principles can be applied more deeply and widely in college or university. If it has not, then the same ground had better be covered there too.

The rest of this chapter is in the nature of soundings. It is my idea of what a study of Jesus at school level might contain. Another man might choose differently. But he, like me, would draw his material from the Gospels. There is nowhere else to draw it from.

I have already suggested that the character of Jesus should be studied as the character of Hamlet would be if Shakespeare's play were set for an examination. Has Jesus a character in this sense? The devout believer has tended to see him, perfect in mind and perfect in body, moving majestically on a course willed for him by his Father and charted for him in the Old Testament, himself as a matter of course making the one ideal response to every situation as it arose, barely reacting individually until he finds himself in Gethsemane.

But his soul was a created soul, finite therefore, the intellect not omniscient, the will not automatically one with the Father's, as he showed in Gethsemane. And his body had reached him, says the New Testament, from a long ancestry, forty generations back to David—how many back to the beginning of the human race? As we have noted, he was not simply Man. He was this individual man, with his own human powers and limitations.

So we study him. We might begin with his way of speaking, not merely to the multitude, sermonlike, but to individuals. Loving-kindness is very far from being the whole picture. His speech is terse and to the point, with no sentimentality at all. Most of what he said would not go very well with most of the statues and paintings.

We are told that he loved "his own" (the Apostles) "to the end" (John 13.1), that he had a special love for one of them, that he loved the family at Bethany, Martha and Mary and Lazarus; that he loved the Rich Young Man who left him "sorrowing because he had great possessions." These are all the occasions I recall. And while we are told that he loved them, we do not hear *him* say so.

Only four or five people do we hear him praise: Nathanael, "an Israelite without guile" (John 1.47); a pagan centurion (Matthew 8.11); a scribe—"You are not far from the kingdom" (Mark 12.34); Mary of Bethany—"She has chosen the better part" (Luke 10.42); John the Baptist—"No man born of woman is greater than he" (Luke 7.28).

It would be a solid gain for the student to consider *in their context* all the sayings of Jesus to individuals. We have referred to "Get thee behind me, Satan," spoken to Peter. Add to that all we are told of his saying to the Twelve, and we are left wondering how he ever decided to build his Church on them. When the Gentile woman begged him to heal her daughter, he asked her if she expected him to feed the bread of the children (the Jews) to dogs. But he did work the miracle. Come to think of it, he praised her, too, for her faith—and partly, at least, for her ready wit (Matthew 15.28).

Then there is the power of his anger. "The harlots shall enter the kingdom of God before you" (Matthew 21.31). "You are like whitewashed tombs . . . full of dead men's bones and all filthiness" (Matthew 23.27). Matthew gives these two in the week between Palm Sunday and Good Friday: they did nothing to save Jesus from death. From the beginning of his Public Life, at least, he knew the death that awaited him; he feared it but never swerved, said and did whatever had to be done, thus only making it more certain. Look especially at the long attack on the Establishment in Matthew's twenty-third chapter. There is no greater passage of invective in all literature.

What it all comes to is that his love was a mightier thing than we have realized. The whole mixture that was himself poured into it. In it he went to his death, praying for his enemies.

But what kind of man was he inside himself? We need to read carefully. He challenges his critics: "Who shall convict me of sin?" Hebrews says that he was tested like us in all things *but without sin* (4.15). Surely those last three words are a surprising postscript to be tossed off so casually. They certainly make some difference to the likeness of Christ's testing to ours! Was he in fact tempted as temptation is known to us? "Tempted" in Scripture usually means "tested" not, as with us, "attracted." Tested he certainly was; but was he in any sense attracted by, and so forced to cope with, some pleasure forbidden because sinful? We could know only if he told us, and he does not.

Indeed he tells us almost nothing, in words, of his own feelings. Again and again he spoke, so very unemotionally, of the death that awaited him. How early he knew of it, he does not say.

Very close to the end he said: "If I am lifted up, I will draw all men to me" (John 12.32), and John comments: "He said this to show by what death he would die." But he had used the same phrase two years earlier at the beginning of his Public Life; very soon after Cana, when he spoke of his being lifted up for the healing of mankind (John 3.14). And he used it once in between. So from Cana to Calvary he walked in the shadow of death. But until Gethsemane he only once expresses any emotion about it, and that emotion was impatience: "There is a baptism with which I must be baptized, and how I am constrained till it be accomplished" (Luke 12.50).

He was speaking of baptism in his own blood on Calvary (as we see from Mark 10.38), and he wanted it to happen (if only to get the strain over?). Yet when it was actually upon him, the blood poured out of him as sweat pours and he begged his Father to let the cup pass from him, if that might be his Father's will. That sweat of blood was a measure of the anguish which had caused him to say "Get behind me, Satan" to Peter, when that impetuous person urged that he must not suffer and die. To return to a question we have already glanced at: Was he asking his Father for what he had called Satanic when Peter urged it on him or is there some element we are overlooking? We must look deeper.

I think the key to understanding lies in Jesus' reference at the Last Supper (Luke 22.37) to a verse of Isaiah which had to be fulfilled in him and was now being fulfilled: "He was numbered among the transgressors" (Isaiah 53.12). The whole verse reads: "He poured out his soul to death and was numbered among the transgressors, yet he bore the sin of many and made intercession for the guilty." Already in the same chapter Isaiah had written: "He was wounded for our transgressions, he was bruised for our iniquities. Upon him was the chastisement that made us whole, and with his scourging we are healed." Peter sums it up for us: "On the cross his own body bore our sins" (1 Peter 2.24).

It is Jesus' reference to Isaiah which shows us, as it had shown Peter, that it was the weight of mankind's sins which constituted Gethsemane's deepest agony. He was not simply asking to be spared suffering and death (which was what Peter had urged upon him). He had accepted to be so identified with the sinful race of men that their sins could become his burden. We have no experience to tell us what such an identification would mean in its actuality. But we are shown something of what it meant to Jesus: "He began to be greatly distressed and troubled. And he said to them, 'My soul is very sorrowful, even to death' " (Mark 14.33–4). The cup was now at his lips. He had known theoretically what it was to be. The reality was beyond all theorizing.

I have taken these three texts—"How I am constrained till it be accomplished," "Let this cup pass from me," "Get thee behind me, Satan"—as an example of how closely we must weigh one part of the Gospels against another. We cannot simply race through them at a hand-gallop. The Gospels are not easy to read. Nor is Jesus.

WHO WAS HE? WHAT WAS HE?

Meeting him in the Gospels, listening to him, we are left in no doubt that he is a man, but there are too many things said and done by him which fall outside human limits. Students should be encouraged to note instances of this sort. I am not thinking of the great special events—the Virgin Birth (told so matter-of-factly by Matthew and Luke that only a failure to see any value in virginity could lead to its rejection), the Miracles, the Foretellings, the Resurrection—but what we may call his daily habit. He is man, but manhood does not wholly explain him, does not wholly contain him.

We note, for instance, his unvarying assumption of something special in himself, something different, something not in other men save inasmuch as he gave it to them. The Sermon on the Mount (Matthew 5 to 8) is full of this assumption. "I have come not to destroy the law and the prophets" (startling enough to his countrymen) "but to *fulfill* them" (perhaps more startling still). He goes on to develop—on no authority but his own—three of the commandments on murder and adultery and false swearing, commandments given by God through Moses. The first reaction of his hearers must have been "Who does he think he is?" We ourselves had better look closely at precisely the same question.

There is the name he gave himself, "The Son of Man" —never used by his followers, and practically vanishing with him. It answered no question, merely showed there was a question to which they must find the answer. It was a strange name with which to claim powers almost all of which exceed man's measure. "The Son of Man has power on earth to forgive sins," "is Lord of the Sabbath," "will be seen at the right hand of God's power," "will come with power to execute judgment."

Only the Father Knows the Son

Phrases like these could only have added to the shocks he had given in the Sermon on the Mount. But he was to speak of another Sonship that was his, incomparably beyond anything the phrase Son of Man could mean. "No one knows the Son but the Father, and no one knows the Father but the Son, and anyone to whom the Son shall reveal him" (Matthew 11, Luke 10).

He is asserting a unique equality of interknowledge between his Father and himself, each knowing the other as no man knows either. It all flows from him so naturally —no hint of originality, no air of saying something that could only be explained by being explained away. It is the kind of saying that we might have expected to find in John's Gospel: we find it in Matthew's and Luke's.

To all who accept him Jesus is clearly Man Plus. The Plus is differently read by different Churches and individuals, but all agree that it lies in the uniqueness of his relation with the Father. He is the God-man, whether those who use the phrase believe him both God and Man, or only a man indwelt by God, possessed by God, inspired by God as no other man ever has been or could be. For us it is the first. He is God the Son, he is man: "God sent his son, born of a woman" (Galatians 4.4). His double sonship—of God, of Mary—matters to us because, as Paul goes on to say, in it we are redeemed, in it we receive the adoption of sons.

At every point what Christ says is the root. What the New Testament writers made of it, what the Church has made of it, what we ourselves are going to make of what Church and New Testament have given us, must grow out of that root.

As I have said, the whole of this study of Christ consists in taking soundings in the Gospels. That is what I have done with the phrases I have been quoting. The teacher will know them all, will know those other, in some ways profounder, phrases quoted by John's Gospel, together with the assumptions of divinity in the Epistles out of which the doctrine of the Incarnation has grown. And he will know the relation between Incarnation and Trinity, the mysterious threefoldness shown to us in Christ's revealing of the inmost life of God.

For the revelation of two selves within the One God did not end what Christ was to show of the Inner Life of God. There was a Third self: the Pneuma, the Breath, which we translate spirit (it might interest the younger ones to know that we use the Greek word in pneumatic drill, to say nothing of pneumonia). To begin to grasp what Christ Jesus is telling us of himself (and ultimately of our own selves) we must see something of his relation to all Three.

Trinity and Incarnation

The Catholic is not forced to claim that the whole of what the Church teaches on Trinity and Incarnation can be found in Scripture—though I'm not saying it cannot! But God is communicating with us through both Church and Scripture and we can safely rely on their harmony— even when an occasional difficulty in harmonizing reminds us that we are dealing with a reality without parallel, into the understanding of which we are still growing, and for whose full utterance human language lacks the resources. The evangelists did not "theologize" or philosophically analyze the God-man reality they had lived with in Jesus and recorded in the Gospels. But the explanation of what they recorded began very soon after, and has never ceased.

In crude summary we can set it out *as the Church has grown with it,* using the opening of John's Gospel as the clue: "In the beginning was the Word and the Word was with God and the Word was God." Since God is a spirit, the Word that is "with him" cannot be one of our sounded words, but a word uttered in the mind, an Idea. And this Idea, John says, *was* God. Idea of what? Of himself. God knowing himself with infinite knowing power, conceives within his own being an Idea (or Concept) of himself. The Idea is totally adequate, by which I mean that there is nothing in the God who conceives the Idea-of-himself that is not in the Idea-of-himself that he conceives! The Idea then is infinite, eternal, omniscient, omnipotent; is God as the thinker is, Someone as the thinker is, a Second Self or Person equal to the First—with a received equality indeed, but an equality wholly given. The Second Self is distinct, for a thought is not its thinker, but is inseparable, since a thought cannot exist save by going on being thought!

I have called this crude: but beginnings tend to be. John himself must have wondered how much he had managed to say. After the opening phrases he says "Son" in place of "Word." And we can see a connection between a thinker uttering his whole being in a word and a father uttering his whole being in a son. Yet we must always remember that both Word and Son are metaphors drawn from human experience: for beings who had no lungs and did not procreate—angels, say—other metaphors would have had to be found. A dozen verses later, John goes back to the Word (*logos* in Greek, by the way): "The Word was made flesh and dwelt among us and we saw his glory, the glory as of the only begotten of the Father, full of grace and truth." His Gospel does not use it again.

It was the genius of St. Augustine which saw Father and Son combining in an utterance of total love, so that the divine nature is filled with their love, and a third self is produced, a self equal to them in all things, since they have withheld nothing that is theirs. Jesus and the New Testament writers call the Third One the Holy Spirit.

Perhaps what most directly affects us in the Trinity is that God's love, like God's knowledge, is Someone, not something only.

In interpreting what the New Testament has to tell of Trinity and Incarnation, the Church—indeed the vast majority of Christians until very recently—makes use of two keywords, Person (*who* one is) and Nature (*what* one is). In Christ there was one Person, God the Son. He had two natures, the nature of God which was his from his Father eternally, and the nature of man, spirit embodied or body enspirited, conceived in Mary's womb. The one same Jesus who said "Whatever I see my Father doing, I do in like manner" could also say "I thirst," "My soul is sorrowful even unto death." It sounds like two different people speaking. Yet it is the same I, which in the first statement asserts limitless power and in the other admits weakness. The least one can say is that one person is operating on two levels. Did anyone but Christ ever use "I" to express both humanity and divinity?

How is this mass of reality to be shown to the young in

such a way that they can know what is being said, grow into it, possess it vitally, be possessed by it? "Grow into it" is the key phrase. It cannot simply be handed to them as a set of formulas to be memorized, then filed away in the back of the mind to be fished out when someone—an examiner, perhaps, or an unbeliever—asks about it. Our Lord did not do that to his Apostles; no one should do it to anyone.

Dogmatic definitions are not blueprints, least of all this of the one Person and two Natures. They widen the area of light, but the light is ringed with darkness all the same. The students must be shown the inevitability of mystery and its splendor.

Mystery

Mystery, we have noted, is the atmosphere in which all must be seen. Seeing reality can be an exhilarating experience; really seeing it includes seeing why we cannot see more of it. To put it in one phrase, we cannot know God as he knows himself, we cannot know one another or even ourselves as well as our Creator knows them and us. Yet the light into which we can grow is life-giving.

The student should be constantly aware that mystery is inescapable: mystery in the form of truths we cannot yet see how to reconcile with one another, mystery in the even harder form of happenings we cannot see how to reconcile with God's goodness—the suffering of animals (which for me is wholly dark) or the possibility of happiness for the saved in heaven while fellow-men are suffering in hell (in which I can see a bare gleam of light).

If we know why we cannot see, the darkness is a kind of light, and we need not be annoyed at not being omniscient. If we accept Christ, we know that he knows every situation better than we do, and has more love in him than we have.

DISCUSSION

It may be hard to persuade the students that discussion of God's inner life is relevant. As I have already said, all one may be able to do at first is show the "structure" of the Trinity as interesting for the mind, like Pythagoras' theorem,

"A linear labyrinth towering
From its perch on the top of a square."

The Trinity may enter their minds not as true, only as a curious idea that Christians hold. But once it is in, it may do its own work upon their minds.

One might begin with the idea everyone has of himself. Your students will admit that the idea we have of ourselves is far from adequate, i.e. we do not know ourselves very well: we discover this afresh each time we do something that leaves us startled at ourself ("I didn't know I was like that"), again when our dearest friend criticizes us. God, simply by being God, naturally knows himself perfectly— why should an infinite God want an inadequate notion of the self he already knows perfectly? So his idea of himself, as we have noted, lacks nothing that he has, is wholly equal to himself, Someone as he is Someone, God as he is God. Yet not identical, but a distinct Person, a second Self.

Get them back to their own self-idea. However much a man may admire, even love, his idea of himself, he does not think of it as returning his admiration, loving him back, so to speak. For his idea is only an idea, something not Someone. But the Father's idea of himself is Someone and can return his love. They can combine in an act of love which has in it all that they have and are. The one Godhead, totally uttered in the Second Person as knowledge, is totally uttered in the Third as love. Three, each wholly God, yet but one God—as a man with an idea in his mind and love in his will is still one man, and would remain so, even if the idea and the love grew to the point of total equality with the man himself.

Can they see it as relevant, having any bearing on their own lives? I have one piece of evidence. In my first ten years of teaching the Faith in the open air, I soft-pedalled the Trinity, concentrated on the one person God. I got nowhere with the crowd. In the forty years in which I taught the Trinity, I made the discovery that nothing gripped the crowd's interest so tight. And this is a point on which a street-corner speaker cannot fool himself. If a crowd is not interested, it goes away. It is easier to hold them on the Trinity than on Civil Rights or even the Spanish Inquisition.

To return to our special theme, the God-man. If the students are encouraged really to think, they may carry the teacher deeper than he had expected into the reality of Christ.

Sinlessness

They will be interested in Christ's sinlessness, for one thing, feeling that if he never committed a sin, then he was not completely human. It is worth dwelling on this. Men do indeed sin: but this does not make them more human, it diminishes them as men. Compare sins with physical defects. All men have some, of various levels of seriousness. But one is not more of a man for having cancer or toothache or indigestion or weak eyes. If there were a man who had no physical defects at all, he would be a more complete man; so would one who had no moral defects.

But why was this man sinless? Was it an incapacity to find any attraction in the forbidden, or only that he could not yield to it? Or did the divinity of his person exercise a continuing veto? These questions arise if the student's mind is in action, and not only his memory. It is right that he should use his mind on them, but always with the awareness that Jesus is not under his microscope or on his psychiatric couch. About other people one may guess. From our experience of life one may feel that the odds are that they will react thus or thus for this or that reason, just as experience shows us that people generally do.

It is rather like applying to man's motives and actions the statistical averages of life expectations and illness and accidents on which insurance companies base their policies. But even these are only averages, with individuals going far higher and far lower. And on a God-man there are no statistical averages, for there has only been one. The only authority on Christ is Christ. And on this matter of his internal response to things men in general find attractive he has not told us.

Knowledge

It is the same with his human knowledge. How much did he know of his own divinity, which includes the question, How much *could* a finite mind know? How early did he know it? What did it mean to him? His manhood was not an appearance, adopted for better communication with men. He was genuinely man, with a finite mind, learning as men learn therefore. The Trinity cannot be known by a finite mind unless God reveals it. How did Jesus' human mind know it? He does not tell us: nor does he tell us how he knew of his own unique Sonship.

Theologians discuss his knowledge under three heads—experimental, prophetic, beatific vision. Of the third we cannot say much at the students' level—it is the direct vision of God, with neither images nor ideas, and they would not gain very much from a discussion of how it could be translated into terms of human experience: in any event we do not, so to speak, catch Jesus using beatific vision in the Gospels. Experimental knowledge, the knowledge which goes with being a man, intellect working on what reaches the mind through the senses, we see in him all the time. And we see prophetic knowledge, given to him (as to the prophets) directly by God with a view to the work he had to do—reading men's minds, knowing what friends and enemies would do, knowing what God willed for himself to do.

The area of his knowledge—did it include modern science, for instance?—he does not tell us: we can speculate if we like. We can say that Einstein's relativity does not seem specially relevant to the work he had been sent to do. But what he does tell us is enough for a lifetime study.

THE MAN JESUS AND THE FATHER

Students might be helped towards growth in intimacy with Jesus by considering what it must have meant to him, at whatever age his human mind came to it, to know that he, the carpenter from Galilee, was the Son of the Father, the Second Person of the Trinity—to know it with the same sort of intellect as ours, to respond to it with an emotional structure like ours. The reverse question—what it must have meant to God the Son that he should be the person, the self, in a human nature—is beyond our gaze (which may not stop us looking).

Prayer

The one thing certain is that whatever may be the duties of a person to the nature that is his, this was one person who could fulfil them with total adequacy. He would, for instance, have been failing in the highest duty if he had not uttered in prayer his manhood's adoration, thanksgiving, petition. Students should consider all the prayers of Jesus recorded in the Gospels. It is clear that God the Son was not simply doing his duty to the human nature he has made his own by expressing what it wanted expressed. He was expressing human thoughts and emotions indeed, but they were his own.

Obedience

For the relation of his will to his Father's, six texts should be looked at specially: "My food is to do the will of him that sent me and to accomplish his work" (John 4.34); "Father, save me from this hour. But no. For this purpose I have come to this hour" (John 12.27); "Father, if thou art willing, remove this cup from me. Nevertheless, not my will but thine be done" (Luke 22.42); "My God, my God, why hast thou forsaken me?" (Matthew 27.46); "Father, into thy hands I commend my spirit" (Luke 23.46); "Though he was Son, he learned obedience by the things he suffered" (Hebrews 5.8).

THE MAN JESUS AND THE HOLY SPIRIT

We remind ourselves that within the Godhead there was already a relation of the Person who was to become the man Jesus to the Holy Spirit. He proceeded from the Father, the Holy Spirit proceeded from him and the Father. As man he was indwelt and guided by the same Spirit of whom as God he was co-producer. His human nature needed light and strength, beyond its own power to provide, as ours does. As man he needed the indwelling of the Holy Spirit as we do. This indwelling he had at every moment. But when some new and special thing had to be done we read of the Spirit's special intervention. At the beginning of his Public Life, the Holy Spirit descended on him in the form of a dove. Immediately after this, Jesus was led by the Spirit into the desert—the Greek word means "thrust," almost "hurled."

At the Last Supper, Jesus gives as sufficient reason for his leaving the world to be with his Father, that if he did not go the Spirit would not come (John 16.17), which casts light upon the comment John had made that "the Spirit could not yet be given, because Jesus was not yet glorified" (John 7.39). The Spirit had sent him into the desert: once he was glorified, he would send the Spirit into the world. On the day of his Resurrection he appeared to the Apostles, "breathed on them and said, 'Receive the Holy Spirit.'" Leaving the world, he told them: "You shall receive power when the Holy Spirit has come upon you, and you shall be my witnesses . . . to the end of the earth" (Acts 1.8).

On Pentecost the Holy Spirit descended on them in the form of tongues of fire, as once on Jesus in the form of a dove.

Acts is the Gospel of the Holy Spirit as Matthew, Mark, Luke and John are the Gospel of Jesus. What Jesus did for the Apostles in his life on earth, the Spirit does for the Church. He does something else. There is an upsurge of the Holy Spirit within the individual, issuing into speaking in tongues unknown to him. There are signs of a return among us of possession by the Spirit. It can only profit from a study of the Holy Spirit in relation to the Son both in himself and in the manhood he made his own.

WHAT JESUS CAME TO DO

Our tendency is to assume that he had come to do whatever we ourselves see as most needed by mankind. There is a mood today in which he is seen as a Proletarian Agitator: but from himself we hear no word of condemnation for either the Roman occupation of his country or the social-economic order. The poisonous root of all exploitation lies in the heart of man. He went direct to the root.

The class should dwell on the half-dozen statements he makes of the reason for his coming. "The Son of Man came to seek and to save the lost" (Luke 19.10)—he said that as his reason for entering the house of Zacheus, a swindling tax-extorter. "I came not to call the righteous but sinners" —this was about another tax-extorter, Levi, who became the Apostle Matthew. Phrases like these link with the name Jesus—"Yahweh saves"—and with the reason given to Joseph for the choice of the name, "because he will save his people from their sins." And all the other reasons Jesus gives flow directly out of them—"to bear witness to the truth," "that men may have life and have it more abundantly": truth and life are the two gifts a sinful world, muddled and devastated, needs.

To Save His People from Their Sins

There is a notion around today that in giving his two commandments of love Jesus was abolishing all other laws, so that the only sin he really objected to was legalism. Against this notion, glance at the list of sins which he says "defile a man," that is make him dirty: "evil thoughts, murder, adultery, fornication, theft, false witness, slander" (Matthew 15.19). The woman he saved from stoning to death for adultery he told to "sin no more"; he said the same to the two paralytics: he was not warning them to be less legalistic in future. The healing of the paralytic at Capharnaum is the only miracle that he said he was working to prove a point, namely that he had "power on earth to forgive sins."

In bringing together a text of Deuteronomy and a text of Leviticus—"Love God with your whole heart and soul and strength," "Love your neighbor as yourself"—and saying "On these two the Law and the Prophets depend," Jesus provided the moral law with a new rationale, a new life principle. All individual sins are ways of failing in the one love or the other, that is what is wrong with them. And that is why he can take sin more seriously than most of his followers do: to the point of attaching eternal separation, from himself and so from his Father in heaven, to a whole series of failures in love of neighbor, all of them being acts of self-love.

To Give Testimony to the Truth

He took sin more seriously than most of us tend to. He took truth more seriously too. "The truth will make you free." Truth is reality as known. Not to know what is true is darkness. We are to "walk in the light," entering into and growing in the knowledge of God and man and human life. Every new thing known about God is a new reason for loving him.

The utterance of religious truth in words is by many dismissed these days as mere statement or proposition: all that matters is "impact"—what truth does to us, the vibrations it causes in us. Impact is necessary, of course: but if we have not studied the actual utterance, we shall not know what has hit us. And without words we shall not be able to communicate either truths or impact to others: it is not enough to vibrate at one another.

THE REDEEMING SACRIFICE

The week from Palm Sunday to Easter Sunday fills a good quarter of the Gospels. In that week, specifically in its last few days, the world was redeemed. How was Redemption achieved? What did it accomplish?

Externally what happened was that a majority of the seventy members of the Jewish Sanhedrin handed over Jesus to the Roman Procurator to be sentenced to death, that the death was by crucifixion, that Jesus rose from death; he moved among his followers for forty days, and ascended to the right hand of the Father. As we have seen, in the two years of his Public Life, Jesus lived in the shadow of this death, in fear of it, but never deviating from the road that led inevitably to Calvary.

Two things particularly must be considered about his

slaying: the first, who did the actual slaying; the second, what it meant—i.e., What in fact did Jesus see himself as doing or undergoing?

1. To find the Jewish people guilty of his slaying is sheerly idiotic, shamefully idiotic. The overwhelming majority even of those living at the time did not know it was happening. The Jews living outside Palestine, greater in number than those inside, could have heard of it only after it had happened. The same is true of those that lived in Palestine—Galilee and Judea—unless they had come up to Jerusalem for the Passover.

What of these last—Jews actually in Jerusalem at the time? We note that the rulers had to (1) "do it secretly for fear of the people making a riot against his killing"; (2) induce the pagan Romans to assume the responsibility. So it was all done at speed—the arrest late Thursday night, the crucifixion round midday Friday. The pressure was put on Pilate by the Sadducees, a rich minority who flourished by co-operating with the Roman conquerors—the High Priests were Roman appointees. In addition we hear a crowd, gathered early in the morning before Pilate's judgment seat, shouting for his crucifixion. How many? Not many, certainly. It could hardly have been more than the five hundred of Jesus' followers by whom, as Paul tells us, he was seen alive after the resurrection (1 Corinthians 15.-6). And that was the whole share of the Jewish people in the crime.

2. What Jesus saw himself as doing we can easily overlook. The key to it is in Luke's account of the Last Supper (22.37). Jesus speaks of a Scripture which had to be fulfilled in him and *was now in fact having its fulfillment.* "He was reckoned with the transgressors"—a verse from the fifty-third chapter of Isaiah. Thus directed by Jesus to that chapter, written six centuries earlier, we find in it the scenario of his redemptive sacrifice. The phrase quoted by Jesus as

now being fulfilled in him goes on: "Yet he bore the sin of many and made intercession for the guilty." Think of other sentences in the same chapter: "He shall make himself an offering for sin"; "He was wounded for our transgressions, he was bruised for our iniquities; upon him was the chastisement that made us whole, and with his scourging we are healed"; "The Lord has laid on him the iniquity of us all."

In his first Epistle Peter sums it up, "On the cross his own body bore" (i.e., took the weight of) "our sins" (2.24).

RESURRECTION AND ASCENSION

These are not just happy sequels to the horror of Calvary. They were the Sacrifice's necessary completion. At Calvary, Christ was not simply a good man being executed by evil men. He was a priest, offering himself as victim for the sinful race of men.

At the Last Supper he had changed bread into his body: "This is my body which is given for you" (Luke 22.19). He had changed wine into his blood: "This is my blood of the new covenant which is poured out for many for the forgiveness of sins" (Matthew 26.28).

All the Old Testament sacrifices for sin had meant the offering to God of a slain victim. The *slaying* could be done by others—the Temple servants, for instance. But the *offering* could be made only by the priest. So it was on Calvary. As priest Jesus offered himself, the victim slain by others.

Calvary was the sacrifice towards which all those earlier sacrifices were feeling. After it there would be no others. It was sacrifice in its perfection. In the Resurrection, God showed his approval of the offering, as never in the prefiguring, by restoring life to the Victim. Beyond that there remained one "completion" never before possible: God actually took to himself the Victim offered to him. What could he have done with a roasted ox or a blood-drained goat? The Ascension was the outward sign of that ultimate completion.

The Resurrection

It was an oddity of Apologetic that Christians continued so long to use the Resurrection as sufficient proof of Christ's divinity—though he himself had given the warning that there are those who would not believe, even if one rose from the dead (Luke 16.31). In fact people today will not accept the Resurrection unless (1) they already believe in Christ's divinity; and (2) they see a meaning in his rising from the dead.

People are suspicious that any happening outside the normal—the Virgin Birth, for instance—has simply been invented to make the hero seem more wonderful. So they dismiss the fact of the Resurrection and concentrate on the meaning—that death is not an end but a beginning. It is true, of course, that the meanings of both Virgin Birth and Resurrection matter enormously. But if neither happened, then the meaning does not arise; there was nothing to mean it, so to speak. One has only buttressed a nice idea with a fairy tale.

The Ascension

With the death on Calvary mankind's redemption was achieved. But Christ's redemptive activity—the application of what was won on Calvary to the race and to each member of the race—continues. "Christ Jesus . . . at the right hand of God intercedes for us," Paul told the Romans (8.34). Hebrews puts this in more detail: "He holds his priesthood permanently, so he is able for all time to call those who draw near to God through him, since he always lives to make intercession" (7.24). He is still priest, offering himself, once slain, now forever living, to his Father for the sins of the world. Of itself Christ's death does not make men holy. It made salvation possible, but each must join Christ in making it actual for himself. What was it that he had made possible?

WHAT REDEMPTION IS

Calvary was an answer to all the ways of man's refusal to be at one with God (hence the word "at-one-ment" which we render unrecognizable by pronouncing it atonement).

The refusal of obedience, for instance, was balanced by "obedience unto death, even to the death of the cross." Man's refusal to give himself wholly to God was balanced by Christ's total self-giving—"Not as I will but as thou wilt," "Father, into thy hands I commend my spirit." Man's refusal to love neighbor as self was balanced by "Father, forgive them, for they know not what they do."

All this happened in his human soul and body. His divinity did not save him from suffering. And the first effect of his sacrifice happened within himself. "He was established as Son of God in power"—*dynamis*—that is, he was established in the existence as man which was proper to the only-begotten Son of God (Acts 10.38). It was not simply conferred upon him by his Father, he had earned it in fear and trembling, as we must earn our share in it. Hebrews 5.9 tells us that by his sufferings he was made perfect. In the man Christ Jesus the self-offering cancelled all that lay between human nature and God. And in some way this means salvation for men: "God in giving life to Christ, gives it to us" (Ephesians 2.5).

I am not one of those who think today's young will see Christ and his work all the clearer if they begin by spending some time on Salvation History in the Old Testament. Christ and revelation history each shed light on the other, but the light Christ sheds is incomparably greater.

This, I think, applies especially to Adam and Original Sin. All my own experience shows that if we begin with Adam we get tangled up in evolution and never reach Redemption at all. Christ's sacrifice has won salvation for men who have never heard of Adam. What he did for us *as we now are* can be stated without reference to Genesis. In the light of what Christ did for its healing, we can consider the breach between the human race and God at the race's origin without risk of confusion.

But if the teacher sees that his pupils read all Our Lord's Old Testament references within context, it will be a good preparation for the study of the Old Testament which should at some point be done.

DISCUSSION

For a great many students any talk of bulls and goats and temple servants may seem like a kind of raving, treating the nauseating cruelties of a long-dead ritual as if it could conceivably matter to us. Remind them that we are trying to find what his own dying meant to Christ. Their abolition meant something to him—four times, I think, he quotes the prophet Hosea's words "Obedience is better than sacrifice": but they lay in the line of spiritual development which led to himself, and through him to the Christian world of today, and in whatever may be in wait for Christ's followers till the world ends.

But apart from that, your students will certainly ask how Jesus' suffering could possibly have brought salvation or anything else to anyone but himself who suffered it.

One has heard Redemption "explained" monstrously, as if Christ had said to his Father: "All men deserve death. Would you mind killing me instead of them?" But that was not the way of it. It was rather as if he had said: "For doing your will, teaching your will, speaking against evil representatives, I am to be killed. Will you accept my death and apply it to all men's needs?" That this request should not be pure presumption depends on his unique personal relation with the Father.

The students will still want to know what possible connection there is between Christ and us which would give sense to such a use of his suffering for our healing. There is mystery here: it simply cannot be stated geometrically. But we can glimpse it, see it in the context of Christ's unique personality, begin to live mentally and emotionally, grow in its light. As in so many matters, not only of religion, we can feel more than we can say, but what we do manage to say can enrich the feeling.

We may approach this particular mystery in two stages:

1. We are in some way identified with Christ in life and death. The identification means that *what is done to us his brethren is done to him.* Jesus had said if you give or refuse food or drink "to the least of these my brethren, you are doing it to me." When Saul, who was to be Paul, was on his way to Damascus to continue his persecuting of Christians, he heard a voice challenging him: "Saul, why do you persecute *me?*" He asked "Who are you, Lord?" And the answer came: "I am Jesus whom you are persecuting" (Acts 9.5).

2. But the mystery went both ways: *what had been done to him was in some mysterious way done to us:* his brethren were mysteriously involved in what he did and suffered. Paul makes a wonderful effort to say the unsayable to the Galatians: "With Christ I am nailed to the cross, it is no longer I who live, but Christ who lives in me." The identification is a reality not a fiction. We have been reborn. By birth we enter into life, by a second birth we enter into a second life. And none of this is mere words. Consider what Our Lord says depends on it: "Unless one is born again of water and the Holy Spirit, he cannot *enter the kingdom of God*" (John 3.5).

Rebirth

For the thirty or forty years before John's Gospel was published, rebirth was seen by the Church as the whole point of redemption. From the kind of men we are by birth we are to be reborn into the possibility of being the kind of man Christ was. From the life of fallen man we are reborn into the life of Christ. Listen to Paul: "Baptized in Christ, we have put on Christ" (Galatians 3.27). "If anyone is in Christ, he is a new creation" (2 Corinthians 5.17). "Put on the new nature created after the likeness of Christ" (Ephesians 4.24).

It is tragic that we drown the meaning of Christ-ened in the pronunciation christened—"crissened," heaven help us. Christening, mispronounced, is thought to mean "naming": whereas it means being built into Christ, made members of him. Would all godfathers and godmothers go as lightheartedly to a Christ-ening as they so often go to a christening?

Life in Christ had been the atmosphere of life in the Church for sixty years before John's Gospel. You find the words "in Christ" all over the writings of Paul and the rest. John shows us Christ emphasizing its reality. "I am the life," he said at the Last Supper. If he had said "I have the life," we could have said "Please give it to us": since he said "I *am* the life," we can but say "Please, Lord, live in us." And that is what he does, but with a special addition— there is to be a two-way inliving, he in us and we in him.

And living in Christ brings us into life-giving union with the Blessed Trinity. At the Last Supper Jesus summarizes redemption: "I in my Father, and you in me, and I in you."

This is all so different from the atmosphere in which they live their daily lives that some of your students may mock at you for saying it—rather like the haw haw of a yokel when he is told that the sun doesn't go round the earth. (He knows it does—he has seen it.) But even the more serious students, to say nothing of ourselves, may find no attraction in it—not enough attraction in it anyhow to drive them to the effort, first of finding out what is being said, then of so living in the light of it and relating their lives to it, that it becomes their natural light.

They can, of course, decide that it is simply not for them—which is like choosing to live in a pre-Copernican world, round which the sun can in good weather be seen to travel every twenty-four hours.

Short of thus abandoning it, they can learn it, put it away in the mind's files, where it can be gathering dust unless something forces them to look at it once more and find that what they had come to remember as part of their childhood's faith is the very light in which a grown man can richly live. Fortunately our everlasting future depends not on what we know but what we love. But it is a pity not to realize to what a degree love can be enriched by knowledge.

Here end our soundings into Jesus himself as we meet him in the Gospels. How much can be taught how early must be for the teachers to decide. At least the young should go out into college or into the world with all of it given to them. Is this an unrealistic ideal? It is not an ideal but a minimum, if the young are to be brought close to Christ Our Lord. If it is unrealistic to try for it, God help us all.

III

Man's Life as Jesus Sees It

This chapter treats of the context of reality in which all must live. Within that context each man lives out his own individual life, with a variousness from one man to the next which would be dazzling if we dwelt on it too long. But the reality *within which* all our so various lives have to be lived is one and the same reality for all. One person differs from another in how much he knows of the texture and shape of reality, and differs again in how much each chooses to ignore of what he does know because he feels he cannot cope with it to his own satisfaction, or at all.

But the fundamental problem for everyone is what life is all about: Why are we here, where are we supposed to be going, how are we to get there? *Above all, How do we know?*

For a man to ask these questions and come to the conclusion either that there is no way to find the answer or no answer to find is a grave misfortune, dooming his life to ultimate meaninglessness, as he must end in being swallowed up by the darkness from which for no special reason he had emerged. But one who never gets round to asking them at all must surely be mentally retarded, complacently living out his life in meaninglessness.

The teacher should try to build these questions into the students' mental structure, so that they never shed them but possess in them a permanent touchstone for the testing of any idea or ideology presented to them. I do not mean build the *answers* into their minds, only themselves can do that. But answered or unanswered, there is health in the very questions, a basis of maturity.

Observe that not only can science not answer the first question of all; no science is even equipped to ask it—why anything exists, why there isn't nothing. Nor can any science tell us what is the point of the whole carnival of existence. The answers can be known only on two conditions:

(1) that the universe is not simply an accident that happened to happen but had a mind and a will at its origin— God, Lord, Elohim, the names are in rich variety;

(2) that the mind has communicated with us. God has communicated in many ways, especially through the Prophets, most richly in Jesus.

Our concern as Christians is with the answer Jesus gives us. And it is not a matter of choosing between his answer and others. There are no others. It is his answer or nothing. Without him there is a cloud over the origin of all things, and nothing as man's goal. For the believer in him there is intelligence and love at man's origin, and fullness of life in union with God as man's goal.

WHY ARE WE HERE?

Jesus accepted the superb insight or revelation uttered in Genesis, developed in the later Old Testament, that God created all things whatsoever by his will to create, needing no pre-existing material to work on. The Old Testament Jews had no word for "nothingness," but would have rejected with horror the suggestion that anything could exist independently of God and his all-power. Everything that exists (they had no word for "existence" either) is held in being by his will. In this "everything" the Old Testament came to see angels good and bad, men living and dead, animals, plants, and non-living matter.

So indeed did Jesus. Any Christian who is embarrassed to find him saying, "Their angels see the face of my heavenly Father continually," or "Satan was a murderer from the beginning," must de-barrass himself as best he can. For many a Christian, indeed, it is just as embarrassing to find that he believes that the dead not only survive—Abraham, Isaac and Jacob are alive *now* (Luke 20.37)—but can be in contact with this world. Matthew, Mark and Luke all have Moses and Elias talking with Jesus on the Mountain of the Transfiguration—Luke says the talk was about the death he was to die in Jerusalem (so that concerned the dead too!).

The Old Testament's main concern is with man, especially in his relation to the God who not only made him but made him in his own image and likeness, made him therefore to love God and his fellow-men, made him to till the earth, fill the earth, dominate the earth. Apart from his will for men, the Old Testament tells little of what we may call God's own life, least of all what we may call his inner life: With what did he concern himself when not keeping the Jews on the right road?

As to the difference Jesus makes to our vision of God, the topic is too vast, libraries would not cover it. As earlier, I can only take soundings. Observe that the God of both Testaments is a personal God—i.e., he knows and loves. The Impersonal Absolute of Hindus and Greeks and any number of modern Christians is not in Scripture: they would make nothing of a God to whom a sparrow's death mattered. The teacher cannot do better than have his students read what the Old Testament has to tell of God's love for men, and God's desire to be loved by them. On all this the Old Testament is as rich as the New.

But, as we have seen, Jesus opened the inner life of God to us as even the Old Testament's spiritual masters had not known it. Only as we come to grasp what he tells of the three selves within the divine Oneness, can we see the profoundest truth about Jesus of Nazareth and the greatest gift he brings to ourselves. For, as he shows, the purpose of our being is to come to the fullness of our humanity in union with Father, Son and Holy Spirit; not only that—we travel the way to that undying union in their company.

WHERE THE ROAD OF LIFE LEADS

So by the will of God we are on the road of life. But a point will come—suddenly if there is violence, otherwise by slow wearing—when the body can no longer respond to the life-giving energies pouring into it from the soul. The body, no longer vivified, falls away into its elements. We are dead. Is death the end?

Jesus says that it is not. It is the end of the road, certainly; but not the end of life, not the end of you, of me. Listen to him: "Do not fear those who can kill the body but cannot kill the soul" (Matthew 10.28). The body's death does not mean death to the soul, the psyche, the life principle in us. He reminded the Sadducees, who denied survival, that Moses had "called the Lord the God of Abraham and Isaac and Jacob," and that "He is not the God of the dead but of the living" (Luke 20.38). On Calvary, Jesus says to the thief dying alongside him, "This day you shall be with me in Paradise" (Luke 23.43)—we know where the two bodies were.

Death is a gateway through which all men must pass. To what? The answer depends on what they have made of their individual *selves*—the selves they started off by being, the selves they have become. If they love God and their neighbor, they go to the place Christ has "gone to prepare," a place of everlasting joy in fullness of life. But if self is what they have chosen, to the exclusion of God and their fellow-men, then self is what they will get eternally, in the company of all who have made the same bleak choice. Bleak it is. For self cannot satisfy: there are too many needs in man that only God and other men can meet. The self-elect have chosen final futility. Jesus makes it clear that life is not just a game, with prizes for the winners and consolation prizes for the losers. He gives no details of life in hell: all the devils-and-pitchforks phantasmagoria is Dante, not Jesus. But he uses the word "fire," and whatever he means by it, he does not mean consolation prizes.

Men themselves make the decisive choice between love and self-love. It is interesting that practically every instance of eternal loss Jesus gives is of failure not in his first command, love of God, but in his second, love of neighbor. It is the disciple whom Jesus loved who states the principle: "If we do not love our neighbor whom we see, how shall we love God whom we don't see?" (1 John 4.20).

DISCUSSION

A road has no purpose, life on it has no meaning, save in relation to where it is leading. It is a kind of half-witted-ness not to try to find out where life's road leads: we'll be a long time dead, the brevity of life is not just sermon stuff.

The materialist asserts that there is no life for us after death, that nothing awaits us but a re-merging into the mindlessness of the matter from which for no ultimate purpose each of us has emerged. He cannot prove this assertion—indeed he usually assumes that it needs no proof: one has only to look: he has seen dead bodies and they look so very dead. But what has he actually seen? Simply the destruction of that in which, when he was alive, the owner of the body had done a myriad observable things

—occupied space, walked, talked, sat, slept, woke, spoke, ate, drank, gestured, laughed. But is that the whole man?

Certainly what we see a man doing is not the whole of his activity—there are all the unobservable things, and they are the governing things. There is his thinking, for instance, and his deciding. No eye has ever seen either a thought or a decision, no nose smelt it, no hand touched it, no palate tasted it. We may feel that at least the ear can hear it. But the ear can hear only the sounds in which the thought was uttered—just as the eye can see the actions in which a decision was carried out, but no eye ever saw a decision.

Certainly no one ever saw any thinking or deciding done by that which he actually sees go into the grave or into the furnace. A materialist may assume that there is no other element in man—the element we call spirit—to account for them, that the body does the whole thing. But it is only an assumption and surely not very probable. Thoughts, we have just noted, have none of the qualities we associate with matter; and the gulf between thought and matter is even wider when we consider so much of what our thoughts contain—general ideas, ideals, philosophical and mathematical systems, moral certainties.

One final point he may make against life after death: the raw material out of which the mind produces thoughts comes to it through the sense organs and the brain. How can it function when our sense organs and brain have gone to dust?

You cannot simply look up a book and produce an answer. All you can do is invite him to think along with you. How in daily life the spirit "reads" the brain, takes over the information there gathered, we cannot clearly see—we are doing it all the time, but we haven't a notion how. We cannot expect to see any more clearly how the mind would function in a disembodied condition which we have not yet experienced. But it is hard to see why it should not "read" the material world as well as it now "reads" that piece of the material world which is the human brain—why should it not take it straight rather than filtered?

I am not offering any of this as proof, but as a way of seeing reality which has plenty to commend it. I don't think it answers everything. But it shows that what can be seen happening to a dead body does not settle the question of what has happened to the man. That in us which does the thinking and deciding is intimately linked with the body that goes to destruction: but is it identical with it? Above all, does it go to destruction with it? Christ Our Lord says it does not. He tells us that, for bliss or woe, there is survival.

But there is another way of attack on survival—namely, to mock the after-life as Christians are supposed to see it. There is Marx's friend Engels sneering at "the tedium of personal immortality." There are Marx's disciples sneering at the joy of the next life as cover for capitalist exploitation in this: "Work all day, feed on hay/ There'll be pie in the sky when you die."

As against this the Christian has his own difficulties—one in particular, namely that he cannot see any joy in heaven to compensate for all the sins he must give up in order to get there! Something inside him stirs as he hears such jests as "The road to heaven is paved with lost opportunities of enjoyment." He finds himself wondering, perhaps, if it might not be possible to get an occasional weekend off from heaven's too perfect bliss.

If he be a believer of a more serious sort, harps and hosannas seem to make an empty climax to the patternless misery and magnificence of life. A philosophical proof that the soul is a spirit and survives will not meet his deepest difficulties. Only what Jesus tells of the next life will do that.

The Heaven of Jesus

The New Testament concentrates on one verb to express the activity of heaven—the verb "to see," which for spiritual beings means primarily "to know." Christ speaks of the angels who *"see* the face of my heavenly Father continually" (Matthew 18.10). Is this true of men too? It would seem so: to Sadducees Jesus said of those "who attain to the resurrection from the dead," that "they cannot die any more, because they are equal to the angels." In any event John and Paul leave us in no doubt. John says, "We shall *see* him as he is"; Paul sets it out in more detail: here below, he says, we do not look directly at God himself, we see him as if in a mirror, "But in heaven we shall *see* him face to face, we shall know him as he knows us" (1 Corinthians 13.12).

This is what the Church has come to call the Beatific Vision, the seeing which makes us happy. With our minds in direct contact with God who is infinite Truth, our wills raised by that contact to a new power of loving, ourselves united with all other beings similarly united with God, we shall at last have reached our own maturity, individual and social. We shall be complete human beings, no longer merely the material out of which life is trying to hammer men and women fully human.

DISCUSSION

For the older students it may be well to look more closely at the direct vision which is the key to what Scripture, to say nothing of the Church, has to tell of heaven. By our natural powers as human beings, we cannot know anything at all by direct knowledge, but always by means of ideas or images. The mind needs a new way of knowing, a new vital relation to reality: we get the first beginning of this precisely in our rebirth into life in Christ. Here on earth this gives our intellect a new relation to God in Faith, our will in Love, both in Hope. But it reaches its full flowering in heaven. The question that matters at death is whether we have the life in us. It is not to be thought of as a passport to heaven, but as the condition of the direct vision of God which is the essential of life in heaven: without it we could not live there.

A believer new to the doctrine may find himself saying, "Is that all?" It sounds very noble, but not very gay. But both John and Paul show the life in its flowering as unimaginably different from its first green showings here on earth—very much as one who had seen only rosebushes could not imagine a rose. Paul warns us that only a fool would try to make a fancy picture for himself of what the risen body will be like (1 Corinthians 15); John says, "It does not yet appear what we shall be," and this must be true of the whole of life hereafter. The one thing certain is that heaven will surprise us.

One of man's greatest glories is his power of action: that will not be reduced to Engels' "tedium of personal immortality," or to any sort of stagnation however blissful! But what will the activity be? At our present stage we cannot even be shown it in any graspable way, any more than a nuclear physicist could explain to a primitive the strange marks with which he is covering so much paper. The feeling we have already referred to that it might be nice to have an occasional weekend off from heaven is comparable to that of a small boy, revelling in his cowboy outfit and unable to imagine what his elder brother sees in girls.

THE ROAD OF LIFE

So Jesus has told us why we are here, in two senses of "why"—by what *cause*, for what *purpose*—God at our origin, God as our goal. What has he to tell us of life on the way? Three things especially:

(1) that he will be with us on it: "I am with you all days till the end of the world," "I am the way";

(2) that the gifts he had come to give for the travelling of the way—truth, life—he will continue to give, but through men: for the preservation of both he founded his Church;

(3) that we must be born again, this being the essence of his answer.

Life

The necessity of rebirth must have surprised his hearers almost as much as his revelation of a Second Self within the divine Oneness. The Old Testament knows nothing of rebirth. To men sure of their own membership of the kingdom of God it could only be a shock to hear that they must be born again of water and the Holy Spirit or they could not enter it.

The second birth means a second life, not annihilating the first or taking its place, but to be lived along with it, until the two lives grow into the harmony of total integrity. The making of that harmony is our life-work: it is what we are here to do: in it we are making the self which will abide eternally.

Theologians have come to speak of *natural* life—the life we have simply by being men, the life we are born into —and *super-natural* life, the life in Christ into which we are reborn. The terms can be misunderstood. But they express a vital difference. Redemption is in them.

In the post-Gospel New Testament, the phrase "in Christ" occurs round fifty times. He is to live in us, and we in him, he had said at the Last Supper.

Of a two-way inliving the example best known to us is a living body and its cells. Paul compares our life in Christ with that of a human body and its parts, Christ himself compares it with a vine and its branches: "He who abides in me and I in him bears much fruit." Either way, the point is made: we are in the stream of Christ's life, members of a body which is, mysteriously and really, his in that he is its life-source; more closely related to one another than by any natural family kinship. Living in him, we are indwelt by Father, Son and Holy Spirit as he was: for the gifts he came to bring, he speaks especially of the Holy Spirit, who within the Trinity subsists as Love.

Discuss carefully with your students the new powers which come with the life—especially Faith, Hope and Charity, by which we are able to accept and love God and look forward to eternal union with him; Prudence, Justice, Temperance, Fortitude, by which we are able to handle ourselves and deal with others as God would have us. They are spoken of as supernatural virtues, and in relation to the life into which all are born they are—without the indwelling of the Spirit, they would be beyond our power. But it is better to think of them as natural virtues of the indwelt man.

Sacraments

We must see the Sacraments as Christ at work in us for the service of his life in us. God made man a union of matter and spirit, spirit embodied or matter enspirited. There is a comparable union in the Sacraments, material things bearing the Holy Spirit. Concentrate especially on two of them: Baptism by which we are born into the new life, the Eucharist as its daily food. Begin with what the Gospels show of their meaning to Christ.

Baptism (from a Greek word meaning to bathe). When Jesus said, "I have a baptism to be baptized with, and how I am constrained until it be accomplished" (Luke 12.-50), he was speaking of the bathing in his own blood on Calvary. So he was again, when James and John asked that they might have the places next to him in his kingdom and he asked if they were prepared to drink the cup he must drink, be baptized with the baptism that must be his (Mark 10.38).

The baptism of water and the Holy Spirit, he told Nicodemus, was the way of rebirth and thus of entry into the kingdom of God (John 3). He said, "He that believes and is baptized shall be saved" (Mark 16.16); commanded his Apostles to take baptism to the ends of the earth till the end of time (Matthew 28.18). The Apostles began their mission by baptizing thousands on Pentecost day. But the baptism of water draws all its effect from the baptism of blood. Paul says: "Baptized in Christ, we have put on Christ" (Galatians 3.27); "Buried with him in his death, rising with him" (Colossians 2.12). If the baptism on Calvary had not happened, there would be no point in the baptism of water.

There is plenty of mockery of Baptism—questioners asking sarcastically what good you do a baby's soul by wetting its head. We might urge them to direct their sarcasm at Jesus and Paul and John and Peter. But we must be prepared to discuss the Sacramental Principle: the body really matters—the spirit is sacred, but so is the body; God, having made us matter and spirit, does not treat us as if we were not. There is no such thing as a religious area, on entering which we must leave our body behind: and we take our body with us not because we have no way of stripping it off and no convenient place to leave it, but because it is as the whole man that each of us worships God.

Eucharist. When Our Lord said, "Unless you shall eat the flesh of the Son of Man and drink his blood, you shall not have life in you," many of his followers left him. There has always been a tendency, even among Catholics, to feel that he could not have meant it.

Today the argument centers on the Real Presence, with meanings found for "presence" which get rid of the notion that in fact we receive his body within ours. But the phrase "Real Presence" is not in the Gospels. What Christ said was "This is my body." Talk of ways of being present while not being actually there, does not touch that phrase. As against "This is my body," two ways of getting rid of the mystery have been found: (a) to find meanings for "body" which would make it not the body in which he lived and moved and hung on a cross and rose into heaven (but it would be hard to get rid of "my blood" like that); (b) to say "This is my body" was a metaphor like "I am the door." Grammatically this will not stand. A metaphor uses the verb *to be* to link a definite individual, not with another definite individual, but with an abstraction. "I am the door" means I am a way of entry. Jesus did not say "I am this door." He did say *"This"* (which he was holding in his hand) "is my body." It is a mystery indeed, but it is a fact, not a metaphor.

Men have tried, without complete success, to find "how" what he was saying could be so. Transubstantiation was a splendid effort, raising questions of its own all the same. But darknesses as to the way of it do not alter the fact that he said it. It *is* a mystery, certainly. But if he was not uttering a mystery, he was uttering a mystification, one which would deceive the majority of his followers for nineteen hundred years—and uttered within hours before his Passion and Death in agony.

It is more profitable to think out why Jesus wants us to receive him thus. And this stares us in the face. By birth we have a spiritual life and a bodily. We have been reborn into a new life, a life which *is* Christ: "I am the life," Christ said. Each life must be nourished by its own kind of food: ideas will nourish spiritual life, but not bodily; meat will nourish bodily life, but would leave us mentally starved. For a life which is Christ, the obvious food can only be Christ himself. And it is Christ we receive, God and man. By consecration the bread becomes his body, the wine his blood. But where either body or blood is, the whole Christ must be, for it is the Risen Christ over whom death has no more dominion.

The Eucharist is not the food of the individual believer alone, as we might think if we had no words save those of Christ himself. It is the food of the whole body. St. Paul sees it so: "The bread which we break, is it not a participation in the body of Christ? Because there is one bread, we who are many are one body, for we all partake of the one bread" (1 Corinthians 10.16,17).

Mass. Being the kind of creatures we are, we find it difficult to keep all the elements of a mystery in our minds at once. We emphasize now one element, now another: the mind finds either/or so much easier to handle than both /and. We smilingly explain that this is the swing of the pendulum. But pendulums go with clocks; pendulous minds are deficient minds. The Eucharist is indeed food and the Mass a community meal—we are there to be nourished. There are those by whom this element is emphasized as if it were the whole.

But the Mass is a sacrifice too, which we are there to offer. As we have noted, Jesus' priesthood continues: in heaven he offers himself once slain, now forever living, to his Father, interceding that what he won for mankind on Calvary should bring all men to salvation. In the Mass the priest, in the power of Christ and by his command, offers the same Christ to the same heavenly Father for the same purpose. The Mass is not another sacrifice: it is Calvary as Christ continually offers it in heaven.

There never were more flat-footed phrases than "going to Mass," "attending Mass." "I'm not going to Mass today because I don't feel like it" is baby talk. Don't feel like what? If you mean you don't feel like sitting in the church, with as much pious devotion as you can force yourself to feel, while the priest gets on with whatever he is doing at the altar, you simply are not talking about Mass at all.

We are there to do something: not only to join with our fellows in the worship of God—though heaven knows this is plenty!—but to join with Christ in offering his sacrifice on Calvary for the salvation of sinners; and our joining makes a difference. If that is what you don't feel like doing today, at least you know what you are saying. It is as if a member of a beach life-saving squad, told that a man was drowning, decided that he didn't feel like saving life today. In the matter of the Mass, feeling is not the point. You don't need to feel like it, you merely have to realize the vast importance of what you are at Mass to do, and will to do it. "Merely," I say, and wonder how I came to use such a word. How many of us even realize that there are sinners who need saving from the evil in themselves, and that our action in Mass can be effective for saving them?

Paul tells us (1 Timothy 2.5) that because there is one Mediator, the man Christ Jesus, our prayers for others can be effective—even for their salvation. "I became all things to all men that I might save all," he says (1 Corinthians 9.21). And he calls on Timothy to do the same (1 Timothy 4.16). The Mediator uses men's aid in his mediating.

DISCUSSION

Two Lives

This matter of rebirth and of two lives to be lived by one same self will be sheer gibberish to many of your students—a double life suggests double-talk. In my own experience, it has often been possible to get Catholics interested in it if only as an idea, leaving it to them to see its practicality for themselves as life goes on. But that means working hard at presenting the idea both as it actually is and in its relation to reality as they actually experience it.

The Catholic we have been describing—with his powers to accept and love God and look forward to eternal union with him, to handle himself and others as God would have him—does not sound like most of the Catholics the student meets; he is only too conscious that it would be a highly retouched portrait of himself. Go back to the two lives in him. The second, we have noted, does not annihilate the first or take its place. The second life, the life of Grace, does not give us a new body or a new soul, it goes to work in the body and soul we have. Paul reminds us that we each carry our treasures of truth and life and union with Christ "in an earthen vessel." The vessel is ourself.

By rebirth we have the gift of Temperance, but we do not simply lose such natural cravings as we may have—lust or gluttony, for instance. We get the gift of Fortitude; but if it is in our nature to evade difficulties, we do not instantly rush to confront them. A naturally pessimistic man gets the virtue of Hope without losing his tendency to pessimism, which may bring him close to despair.

To quote myself: "Grace gives us power to act virtuously for the love of God. But it does not remove our natural habit of acting sinfully for the gratification of self. There is a war within us, two sets of habits in conflict, now one on top, now the other. Every man's problem is to bring his natural and supernatural habits into harmony." The difficulty for all of us is that the allure of virtue is so very resistible.

Penance

By Baptism we are reborn into the life. The Eucharist is the life's daily bread. But the life can be lost by a deliberate choice of self as against the love we owe God and our neighbor. For this Christ established a way of forgiveness and restoration—a sacrament by which the sinner receives a new inpouring of the life he had rejected.

Penance is a sacrament which uses not a material object like bread or water or wine or oil, but a human situation —one person giving his confidence to another as a patient gives his to his doctor. It is worth reminding the class of the healing of the paralyzed man at Capharnaum, which as we have noted was the only miracle Christ worked to prove a particular point—namely, that the Son of Man had "power on earth to forgive sins" (Luke 5.24). That power is as necessary now as then. He still exercises it through his priests (John 20.23).

We must look carefully at the notion of the Sacrament of Penance as a means of reintegrating us with the Christian community. With the community as inlived by Christ, the body through which he continues his work among men, we must indeed be reintegrated. But people talk as if our reintegration were to be not with God or with Christ but with the men and women of whom the community on earth consists. As such it won't do. How integrated with God or with God-made-man is that community—our own parish, for instance? On the average, is it integrated with Christ any more than we are ourselves? For it and for us, God is the integer, and Christ the way to integration with him.

The students should be warned that sacraments do not work automatically against sin. They do not in themselves make sin less attractive. Catholics sometimes feel that the way to conquer a strong temptation is to multiply confessions and communions: when they find themselves still sinning, they feel that the Sacraments have failed them. But Sacraments are there for the strengthening of the life of Grace: they do not work directly upon the bad habits we have by nature. These can be conquered only by ourselves fighting against them, falling maybe, rising and resuming the battle. If we make the best effort we can, then the reborn life has its own way of operating in us. Living the life as fully as we can, gaining light from the truths, nourished by the Sacraments, men find the ways of action proper to the life gathering strength. Above all, they find themselves seeing Christ closer and clearer.

So we are back to seeing, to that other of Christ's gifts, the truth, after so long a dwelling on the life. To be nourished is one need of the Way, that we may have the strength for the efforts and resistances it calls for, and not simply fall by the wayside. To be illumined is the other, that we may know what the Way is and how to walk it.

TRUTH

Leaving this earthly life, Jesus gave the Apostles the commission for which he had been training them. They were to baptize—we have discussed that; and they were to teach all nations till the end of time. Teach what? Whatever he had commanded them. One problem we have already noted: what he had given them to give the world is nowhere set out for us. It is not in the Gospels or in the rest of the New Testament—not the whole of it, not even the basic instruction given to the new converts. The Apostles knew what it was, and all the teaching of the Church has grown out of that original mass of knowledge.

Teaching, of course, does not mean learning by heart, repeating accurately and drilling others in the repetition. The word of God was not given to us embalmed, our only duty to keep it sacred. It is a growing thing, whether we think of minds growing in it, or of itself seen deeper as minds are used to see it. For it is to be lived by: and the human mind is so made that it cannot be given truths to live by and not think about. It had to be lived up to, it had to be prayed; coming to Gentiles of a totally different religious tradition, it had to be re-expounded; as the centuries went by, new situations arose, whole civilizations indeed, to which it had to be applied: and all the time, growth in the knowledge of man and the universe by way of history and philosophy and science made possible a richer understanding of God: we shall not know God here below as Jesus knew him: but we know things about the creation and therefore about the Creator unknown to the men to whom Jesus had to utter his teaching.

The thinking began early, the principal problem clamoring for quick settlement being how much of the Mosaic Law was still binding. Then came the resemblances to and differences from the Paganisms—the Mystery Cults, Gnosticism and the rest. No religion has stirred the human intellect so mightily into action. And so tumultuously.

Tumultuously is the signature word. Minds of every degree of power from brilliant to half-witted, of every level of character from sanctity to lunacy (among lunatics the religious lunatic has always held the primacy), poured their ideas into the air. Today's sky is thick with the theorizing of the ages, coruscating with today's latest insights. How in all this are we to know what Christ wanted us to have? No one could know the whole of it. It needs to be checked against the truth already known, it must be sifted and channelled that it may reach the ordinary Christian. Otherwise it must remain a glittering chaos.

Christ gave his revelation only because he saw that men needed it: to have left it to men to get whatever meanings they might out of it would have been hardly sane. If the revelation was worth giving, it was worth guarding. Jesus provided for this not by putting limits round the truths to be taught but by guarding the teachers to whom he entrusted them. That was his formula.

"I Am With You"

We had seen it in his last year among us, when he sent out the seventy-two disciples with the almost unbelievable

endorsement *"He that hears you hears me"* (Luke 10.16).
Almost at the end, sending the Apostles to bring his gifts
of life and truth to all nations, he added *"And lo, I am with
you till time shall end."* Just before his Ascension he told
the Apostles that they should be "his witnesses . . . even to
the end of the earth," *when the Holy Spirit should have
come upon them*—the Spirit who, he had promised at the
Last Supper, "would lead them into all truth."

How has it worked out? Had he simply fenced round
the truths, saying This you shall teach and not beyond, it
would have meant a hobbling and inhibiting of the mind.
As it is, all reality, Scripture included, lies open to exploration. The mind may move about freely. But it is always
open to the Bishops, successors of the Apostles, or the
Pope, successor of Peter, to intervene, saying: "This is con-
trary to the revelation" or "This belongs within it."

Not every official intervention is guaranteed by Christ.
He chose to build his Church of men, with defects of intelligence and defects of will: the theologians who do the ex-
ploring can wander down strange byways, the authorities
who pronounce judgment on them can misjudge situations
as Peter did when, under pressure from Jewish converts,
he gave up eating with Gentile converts, and Paul "with-
stood him to the face" (Galatians 2.11). In the daily running
of the Church there is no guarantee of infallibility. But
from time to time, a score of times may be throughout the
ages, we do have an infallible pronouncement: some element of the revelation of Christ is "defined" by Pope or
General Council—that is, an interpretation is officially
given, what is offered to our Faith is stated without error.

It may seem that I am attaching too much importance
to the rituals and formulas of solemn definition. The key is
in the word "solemn": the original statement has been
examined, the Christian experience of living by it and the
work of the theologians tearing one another limb from
limb—all this has been weighed. Only thus is the Church

prepared to commit her Founder and herself. Christ sees to it that his Church is not misled.

No human form of words could contain the infinite, and if it could no human mind could extract it! No statement could end the human mind's growth in it. John's "The word was God . . . and the word became flesh" was a milestone. So was the One Person in Two Natures of the Council of Chalcedon in 451. So are all the definitions—milestones, on a road which will not end till "we shall see him as he is."

It is the nature of definitions to be inadequate compared with the whole reality to be uttered. Inadequate but essential: we know where we have come from, which is a great aid to knowing where we are going. We are not forced to start every exploration of God and his Christ as if no one had ever explored before. The definitions map the territory already conquered by the mind: we can move out from there into the surrounding dark. The discovery of the meaning of revelation by living it is for all of us. Its development by bringing the intellect to bear on it is mainly for theologians. Between the theologians and the magisterium—that is, the teaching authority of the Church—there is bound to be difference. It is worth the ordinary Christian's while to understand why.

Today the difference is at crisis point, with theologians disciplined by the Curia making the headlines. The whole mind of the day is against authority as fettering to the free intellect. Magisterium, we tell ourselves, means mastery, authority means coercion, bad words both of them. In fact magisterium means "the right to teach," authority is from a Latin verb "to increase," and in teaching means "entitlement to be believed." Coercion is not in the meaning of either word: it is simply someone's judgment as to how truth needs protecting.

The creative theologian, devoting the whole of his life

to his study, thrusts excitedly on, in love with his discovery. The magisterium, with the whole of the Church's life to consider, may be less enthusiastic about his new idea: it has to weigh its bearing on the rest of theology and Scripture, on the mind of the great mass of Catholics. The thinker rages that "the Church" prefers authority to truth, the public remembers Galileo.

Looking back over the ages with hindsight to aid us, we feel sometimes the Curia was mistaken, sometimes the thinker. In revolutionary times the Curia may exaggerate the need of caution, at all times the thinker may exaggerate the value of his insight. Either way no great harm was done: truth has been delayed recognition perhaps, but not permanently lost.

What we are facing here is one example of a larger tension, the tension between the spirit and the institution. Each needs the other—without the spirit there is a kind of hardening of the arteries, without the institution the gains of spirit are tossed to the winds. Yes, each needs the other. But each feels the other as a threat. If only the theologians and the Curia would see each other's necessity and sympathize with each other's difficulties.

To me there is an analogy between *monogamy* as reconciling the turbulence of sex with the ordered life of the family, and *authority* as the only way to reconcile the free action of the intellect with the preservation of truth. The Church prefers authority not to truth, as some of its critics complain, but to chaos; values authority not for its own sake but for the sake of the treasure it guards. One unhappy result of our present troubles—or maybe it is not their result but their cause—is that the truths are no longer thought of as treasure.

They are undervalued by the type of avant garde of whom we have already spoken, who disdains meaning and banks everything on "impact"—the positive vibrations set up in ourselves which for him *are* the religious experience.

But the devout Catholic has his own way of undervaluing them. Often enough he has no urge whatever to study them. He is delighted that the Church has all the truth, but is not greatly interested in the truth he is so delighted that the Church has. He is content to leave the great dogmas to the theologians as no concern of his: which means that whatever light and nourishment are in them are not there for him. Or he may memorize the formulas without ever getting at the richness within, which is as if he swallowed walnuts without breaking the shell. Either way he is unequipped to bring Christ's great gifts of truth and life to others. Indeed one test of the value we set on the gifts Christ wants men to have is our attitude to the millions starving for want of them.

If we are never moved to bring them to those others, a real question is raised as to how much they mean to ourselves. If there were a bread famine, we should work night and day for its relief. But this famine is only of the Bread of Life.

Christianity is what religion through the ages has been —an initiation into divine mysteries. If the teacher forgets this, there is a non-class. But however hard the teacher tries, there is a hard shell of resistance to be broken through. Even willing students can accept the formulas but give no further thought to them, live much like everybody else, with more effort to live morally and with the commanded amount of ritual practice, but Faith reduced to obedience (in the sense of refusal to deny). One has heard this attitude compared to that of an eccentric millionaire, who owns a palace but chooses to live in the cellar.

IV

What the World Can Do to the Faith*

Education is a preparation for life, we remind ourselves. Religious Education is a preparation for life with Christ. Always in the religion teacher's mind is the threat of what life in the world is going to do to such relation with Christ as his students may have. By the time they leave school, he has given them, he hopes, what is in him to give about Christ. But he must also have given them his understanding of the world into which they and Christ are going out together. From this angle he must study the world as he studies Christ. I am not thinking of the direct attack, the direct objections, which will be continually hurled at them. What I have in mind is the testing to which life as such will subject them, the "infection of the world's slow stain."

I have spoken of what life is going to do to the students. In fact it is already doing it: the skilled teacher can see it happening. But in the first place the pressure of life is only beginning, and in the second the pupil in a Catholic school can be in more continuous contact with revealed truth

*And the Flesh and the Devil.

than he is ever likely to be again. Out in the world the mighty realities he has learnt about—Trinity and Incarnation, Infinity and Eternity—melt away into the background with so little to keep them vividly present to him. They are not part of the scaled-down world in which we do our daily living—husbands and wives and in-laws, friends and enemies, people we work with and for, financial pressures, politics, sport, pleasures and pains, emotions and appetites—such a full life, so totally secular.

Almost unawares we can slip into living in the mental atmosphere of the age, with only a tincture of Christ to add a comforting illusion of spiritual vitality. I shall not attempt here to look in detail at the myriad ways in which the world will be eroding whatever intimacy with Christ the student may bring with him from school. That will be for each teacher to distil from life as he has lived it himself and seen others live it. I shall look at what seem to me the five main fields in which lie dangers to the student's faith in Christ: money, sex, suffering, the hiddenness of God, and the Church itself (for the Church, as he was taught in school, truly is Christ's Mystical Body, but as he meets it in daily life he can feel it a pain in the neck, and we have such very sensitive necks).

These five have their separate ways of weakening attachment to Christ. With *money* it is a kind of erosion: love of money tends to take possession of a man, he tries serving God and money, but the service to God can dwindle to lip-service: money exacts more than lip-service. With *sex*, it begins with separation from the Sacraments. With *suffering*, one's own or others', it is resentment against a God who allows suffering to continue when surely he could stop it. With *God's hiddenness*, there can be a growing question whether God is there at all. With the *Church*, the failure of such of its leaders as he meets to live up to the principles of its Founder as he sees them can make a man question the value of their testimony to Christ.

In all five fields the religion class should prepare the students for what the world may do to their Faith.

Money

Paul calls love of money a root of all evil. Jesus, I think, rates it as the worst of vices. We remember the money changers he scourged, we remember the camel and the needle's eye! "If you serve money, you cannot serve God" —he says that twice. Can a rich man be saved? Jesus gives the grim answer "Nothing is impossible to God" (Matthew 19.26). The time and energy that go into making money and keeping it occupy the mind to the neglect of its higher powers. Jesus says, "The cares of the world and delight in riches choke the word so that it proves unfruitful" (Matthew 13.22); that is, wealth sterilizes. "They are stifled by the cares, riches, pleasures of life and never reach maturity" (Luke 8.14).

I have not heard much emphasis laid on the Parable of the Rich Fool (Luke 12) who had congratulated himself on the wealth he had accumulated: But God said to him: "Fool, this night your soul is required of you. And the things you have piled up, whose will they be?" Throughout Christ's teaching nothing is clearer than the transience of our life on earth. The earthly things we value may be valuable or worthless, either way they will pass. But how well or ill we have loved and served God and our neighbor will matter eternally: the self we have become, by things well-done or ill-done, will live on forever. This life is a road, not a dwelling place.

It is possible that in these warnings about the dangers of wealth, Jesus had in mind the Church he was founding. Had ecclesiastics taken them to heart, the great breakaway at the Reformation might never have happened. It is at least interesting that the first sin we find committed in the new Church was the lie Ananias and Sapphira told about money.

The young will listen to you about all this, some cynically, some receptively. But even the most receptive will find the charms of money hard to resist as life goes on: they are so very evident, heaven so very remote. And we who teach them will have to examine our own practice in the matter if we are to be even half-convincing.

Sex

Sins in this area are not the worst of sins, but practically everybody is tempted and no other sin creates so urgent and continuous a craving. The young, boys especially, see the promise of all bliss in it (which, as any rational older man can assure them, just ain't necessarily so), all mastery and maturity and virility in promiscuity (but there is no virility in a craving, no maturity in being unable to say no, no mastery in being mastered). Christ's judgment is quite clear. He places the misuse of sex in the list of sins which "defile a man"—i.e., render him dirty—"evil thoughts, murder, adultery, fornication . . ."

In the Sermon on the Mount Our Lord has said "Every man who looks at a woman lustfully has already committed adultery with her in his heart." Notice that "looks at": for he continues "If your eye cause you to sin, it would be better to pluck it out and enter eternal life with one than be cast into hell with two." In fornication "a man sins against his own body, which is the temple of the Holy Spirit" (1 Corinthians 6.18, 19). That is Paul's translation of Christ's word "defile." In the same chapter his list of those who "will not inherit the kingdom" begins "fornicators, idolaters, adulterers, homosexuals." For nineteen centuries the Teaching Church has not deviated from the teaching that sexual union belongs inside marriage, where alone it can serve the new life. But with the present collapse of sex standards, it is necessary to show the young *why* it is right within marriage, wrong outside.

An immediate consideration is that the very complex interrelated sex mechanisms of men and women would simply not exist if they were not meant to have children: their connection with generation is as obvious as that of the lungs with breathing, or the heart with the blood's circulation. Inside marriage not every bodily union is intended for child-bearing, but at least it serves the children already born, serves the whole institution of the family, by making the marriage a warmer, more loving reality: whereas, used outside marriage, the sex mechanism loses all connection with that child-bearing but for which human beings would not have had it.

A profounder consideration is that bodily union is the only human action which will produce living beings, made in God's image, destined for everlasting life. Procreation is pro-creation, deputy creation, a share in God's creative action. It is not only that by it men and women co-operate with God, but that without their co-operation he will bring no more human beings into existence. It is a sacred act, and must not be used in ways he has forbidden. The students may very well laugh at the notion that the act is sacred: but the idea may abide with them and some day bear its own fruit.

A popular line at the moment is that sexual union before marriage or outside it is the highest expression of love. It certainly is not. Love always has as its main meaning the service of the other. In copulation there is too much self-love for love's perfection: the self is too often reduced to a bodily craving, the other to a convenience for the relief of the craving. The Scottish poet Robert Burns, himself pretty much given to free-love, says:

> "It hardens all within
> And petrifies the feeling."

There is a sex paradox which is worth thinking over. To sex is entrusted the continuance of the race—sex being the most turbulent of man's powers, whereas the new life needs the utmost security. In the marriage of one to one lies the answer to the problem—sex love at its most intense, the child brought to maturity. Sex at its most intense? It would be truer to say that only in the total giving of one to one is sexual union even possible. For sexual union is not the union of bodies, it is the union of two selves expressed in the union of bodies—both bringing to the act the whole of their lives, emotions, cares, in a total surrender each to the other. Those who have never made that surrender have never had sexual union, but in the union of bodies remain to the end uncleanly virginal.

All this can be discussed with the older students, who will hardly need encouragement to speak their feelings freely. They are at a difficult age—at least the boys are, for whom alone I can speak. They must be helped to find some kind of middle ground between carnality lightheartedly indulged at one end, despair over failure at the other. I have known cases where masturbation, treated too ferociously in the confessional, has meant cutting off from the Sacraments and ultimately from the Faith. At least they can be reminded of Christ's love for sinners, of the seventy-times-seven of his measure of forgiveness, and of the words he could still find for sinners in the depth of his own agony —the spirit is willing and the flesh is weak.

Suffering

The objection sounds so wholly unanswerable: If God *cannot* prevent suffering, he is not all-powerful. If he *will not,* he is not all-loving. Like all epigrams, it gets its neatness by leaving out too much. It has to be looked at more closely.

Begin by asking what causes suffering, since this is what God is blamed for not dealing with. Suffering comes either from our own collision with the laws of reality or from the effect of the wrong other men do.

There have to be laws, or the universe would not function at all. Without the law of gravity, we should be swept off the earth's surface; without fire's power to burn, civilization could barely have begun. Given our combination of ignorance and folly, selfishness and the rest, we are certain to find ourselves colliding with one or other of reality's laws —a man falling out of an airplane will find the law of gravity working against him, a man who falls into the fire will get burnt. Our lungs may be unable to handle air properly for service of the body; a baby may be born with a damaged brain or venereal disease because of some earlier breach of reality's laws which the breaker of the law may not have known about.

The "collision" may be in the mind—craving for something one cannot have, a woman perhaps. A man may be unable to have her because she dies (physical law) or she can't stand the sight of him (psychological law) or she has a husband (moral law). In face of the moral law one may think one is free; after all, the man could take her if she is willing: but he would only have turned from one wrong relation with reality (wanting what he shouldn't have) to another (taking what he shouldn't have). He may have eased his own craving, but has the mass of suffering been reduced or only shifted?—to the woman's husband perhaps, or to her children; in any event, to society as a whole whose well-being depends upon a stable family life.

Clearly you could hardly have God abolish laws—if the same physical causes could not normally be relied on to produce the same effects, nothing could function at all, nor without rules for the handling of ourselves and other people, could society continue: one might alter the rules, but that would merely mean different rules to collide with!

The only other course is to have God intervene every time the action of any law would hurt anybody. Miracles, of course, do happen. But they cannot become the rule. If life were run by myriads of special interventions, then we could not handle our own lives but must just let ourselves be handled. If every time the strong attacked the weak God intervened, then criminals and victims alike would be toy pieces on a chessboard. Maturity for the individual and the race lies in learning to co-operate with the reality of the universe, and in learning to cope with the evil in others and in oneself.

So far I have merely looked at the great mass of human suffering which arises from collision with the way reality is. There are, of course, natural catastrophes with which collision cannot be avoided—tidal waves, earthquakes, volcanic eruptions. The thing we can be sure of is the loving intelligence behind the universe—no one will suffer permanently for what is not his own fault. There is always a next life. The child dying after a month of agony will be as sure as Paul was, while still suffering, that there is no comparison between the agony and the joy.

The unbeliever is maddened by our bringing in of heaven and the love of God, as if we had produced an ace from up our sleeve. But we cannot be expected to "justify" God's running of the universe without reference to what he himself tells us he means to do hereafter.

God's Hiddenness

The Old Testament does not answer today's universal question: How do we know there is a God? It hardly seems to have occurred to the Old Testament writers: one wonders if they had ever met an intelligent atheist. It must be considered in class, not only because the students have already been faced with it and in the world into which they go from school they will never be allowed to forget it, still more because under the pressure of life God may become less and less real.

There is no doubt that in the last couple of centuries Apologetic, the proving of God's existence by reason alone, was overdone. Only recently does it seem to have re-dawned on our elders and betters that to *show God as what he is* (which includes what difference his existence makes to us), is more likely to win men's acceptance than to *show him as the conclusion of an argument.*

But of course the reaction went too far. From too many schools Apologetic vanished, leaving the students tongue-tied and helpless before the materialist. Even if Apologetic were only defensive, it would be important: there is a lot to be said for not losing arguments. For the believer to be flattened in every discussion is not only discouraging for himself but bad for the unbeliever too—he will not have heard the "case" for God, and will go gaily on looking for more believers to flatten. There is no need to lose the argument. Indeed there should not be an argument. Simply try for a meeting of minds with the unbeliever, you and he each saying what he holds about the origins of the universe.

Even quite young children can see that if something happens, then either somebody meant it or nobody did. If nobody did, it is an accident. There's no point in asking what an accident *means*, accidents are things that just happen. No point either in asking its purpose. The whole point of an accident is that there is no point. It is simply a mess that happened to happen. A mess the universe certainly isn't, so magnificent is its order, and so incredible the interlocking of its parts over so many trillions of light years, so many trillions beyond trillions of miles, all functioning at speeds beyond imagination. Anyone who can believe it all simply happened that way can believe anything. Or rather he can say he can.

For the more sophisticated we may find what caused the universe a more acceptable starting point than who meant it. State the best known of the Christian lines of thought, the so-called argument from contingency—not as an argument but as the way you see it. In daily experience nothing comes into existence without a cause. But if this were universally so, if everything whatever had to depend for existence on something else having happened, then the process could never have got going at all—what something else *is* there outside of everything? Do not expect everyone to grasp this at first telling. It has to be lived with. But with patience the teacher can help the class to face the question: If everything whatsoever had to receive existence, where would existence come from, what source could existence have? A universe with nothing in it but receivers of existence is unthinkable.

The Christian (not only he, of course) sees the source of existence in a being that simply exists, exists in its own right, dependent upon no other thing, having all its reason for existence within itself. This being we call God. It must have a rich fullness of existence, for there can be nothing in the universe—life, power, mind, knowledge, will, love— that does not derive from it. Therefore the word "it" is misleading, these are the attributes not of something, but of Someone. We call that Someone God.

Put all this to the other man, not as a proof, but as the way you see it. Ask him to compare it with his own idea of a universe which simply happens to be there for no reason at all, whether in what it is or external to it. *Either way, something beyond our understanding is at the origin of the universe.* Even if he thinks his view no more of a mystery than ours, he cannot deny that ours at least sheds light on what follows, his sheds none. Our view that intelligence and will are at its origin explains more of the complex interrelatedness of our universe than his notion that it was produced by mindless atoms bashing about through billions of years.

The teacher should not embark on this line of statement unless he sees it so himself: if he does, he must be constantly thinking out ways of saying it more clearly. Nor must he be impatient with students who just cannot see it. I have met people whose faith in God and love of God I envy, who cannot see it; their minds seem not to be built that way.

Clearly as I see it myself, it does not happen to be my way of coming to the certainty that God exists. Before I ever heard it, I believed in him. I had had close on twenty years of knowing Christ in his Scriptures and in his Church. His certainties had become mine—proved right when I lived up to them, proved right when I went my own way against them. His God is my God. All the same I am grateful for those who showed me reason's case for God's existence. It shed new light upon God as creator, and upon man—as created by him out of nothing and held in existence solely by his will.

The Church

The Church as we meet it can be a trial to the Faith, especially to the faith of one not rightly or deeply grounded in it. Ecclesiastics from highest to lowest can strike us as arrogant, power-loving, money-loving. To take a single instance: in place after place we see the rich sought out and honored by the Church authorities as never by Christ. All this is true, but to be shaken in Faith by it means not to have understood what Christ had in mind when he entrusted his gifts of Truth and Life to the Apostles. By that choice of his, healing is brought to us through men who themselves need it; we are helped in the saving of our souls by men who have no guarantee that they will save their own; we ask absolution in confession from men who themselves ask absolution in confession. For us and for them, Jesus is the whole point.

To complain that ecclesiastics are defective in intelligence or idealism is naive. It was Jesus' decision to work upon humanity from within it, not some special humanity made for this purpose, but humanity as it actually is: and his working in it is as real as the humanity in which he works. Just after the Transfiguration and just before giving the Apostles the commission to teach all nations till the end of time, he cried out to a group of them: "How long can I bear with you!" He had said that even when they had done all that was commanded, they should still see themselves as "unprofitable servants" (Luke 17.10). Earlier in that same chapter he had said: "Scandals are sure to come, but woe to him by whom they come."

My own feeling is that students should be prepared in school for the unattractive elements they are liable to meet in the Church. It is for schools to decide how much should be taught and at what age. In my own teaching of unbelievers in parks and on street corners, I never talk about the Papacy without telling of some of our less admirable popes. So my hearers understand why I insist that nothing a pope could do or say would make me think of leaving the Church. I entered it by baptism in Christ (not in the Pope), I remain in it in order to be in Christ's companionship (not the Pope's), a member of his Body (not the Pope's). If a given pope behaved badly, I should sympathize with Christ, whose work among men the pope's ill-behavior was damaging (which is an unhappy reminder of how often our own behavior has dimmed the face of Christ for those who know us). Meanwhile, whether I agree or disagree with Papal or Conciliar policy, I know that in the Church I have the possibility of union with Christ, and so with Father, Son and Holy Spirit and ultimately with my fellow-men, to the very limit of my own willingness.

Some Further Reading

Christ in the Classroom has concentrated on Christ Our Lord. But to know him we must study both the God from whom he came and the New Humanity which comes from him. The author has written about both in the following books:

Theology and Sanity: a survey of Catholic Theology—not a Summa, a summula perhaps. ($3.50, 407 pp.)

Society and Sanity: God and Man being what they are, how should life, individual and social, be lived? ($3.50, 274 pp.) o.p.

God and the Human Mind: God's self-revealing and what men have made of it. ($5.00, 301 pp.)

To Know Christ Jesus ($5.00, 378 pp.)

What Difference Does Jesus Make? ($6.00, 242 pp.; Paper, $2.95 OSV)

Genesis Regained: Creation and Fall related to (1) the myths of Egypt and the Middle East, (2) modern evolutionary theories, (3) man's present condition. ($4.95, 182pp.)

The following passages from these books may shed light on *Christ in the Classroom:*

CHAPTER I

Mystery *GTHM* 18–39
Spirit *GTHM* 40–63
Intellect and Imagination *T&S* 12–18, 24, 36–9, 49–53

CHAPTER II

Scripture and Church *GTHM* 89–133
The Man Christ Jesus *WDDJM* 17–53, 75–93, *T&S* 166–220
God the Son *WDDJM* 212–220, 231–241